Table of Contents   *Page*

Introduction

Introduction...1

Summary Tables

Summary Tables..2

Discretionary Eliminations and Reductions

Department of Agriculture

Conservation Operations..9
Forest Service Land Acquisition..10
McGovern-Dole International Food for Education..11
Rural Business and Cooperative Service..12
Rural Development Salaries and Expenses..13
Rural Water and Waste Disposal Program Account..14
Single Family Housing Direct Loans...15

Department of Commerce

Economic Development Administration..16
Manufacturing Extension Partnership..17
Minority Business Development Agency..18
National Oceanic and Atmospheric Administration Grants and Education.........................19

Department of Defense

Base Realignment and Closure...20

Department of Education

21st Century Community Learning Centers..21
Comprehensive Literacy Development Grants..22
Federal Supplemental Educational Opportunity Grants..23
Federal Work Study..24
Gaining Early Awareness for Undergraduate Programs..25

Impact Aid Payments for Federal Property..26
International Education..27
Strengthening Institutions..28
Student Support and Academic Enrichment Grants..29
Supporting Effective Instruction State Grants..30
Teacher Quality Partnership...31
TRIO..32

Department of Energy

Advanced Research Projects Agency - Energy..33
Advanced Technology Vehicle Manufacturing Loan Program and Title 17 Innovative Technology Loan Guarantee Program...34
Applied Energy Programs...35
Mixed Oxide Fuel Fabrication Facility Termination..36

Department of Health and Human Services

Agency for Healthcare Research and Quality..37
Community Services Block Grant..38
Food and Drug Administration Medical Product User Fees..39
Health Professions and Nursing Training Programs...40
Low Income Home Energy Assistance Program..41
National Institute for Occupational Safety and Health..42
National Institutes of Health Topline...43
Office of the National Coordinator for Health Information Technology.............................44

Department of Homeland Security

Federal Emergency Management Agency State and Local Grants.......................................45
Flood Hazard Mapping and Risk Analysis Program..46
Transportation Security Administration Law Enforcement Grants....................................47

Department of Housing and Urban Development

Choice Neighborhoods..48
Community Development Block Grant...49
Grants to Native American Tribes and Alaska Native Villages...50
HOME Investment Partnerships Program..51
Rental Assistance Programs...52

Self-Help and Assisted Homeownership Opportunity Program Account..53

Department of the Interior

Abandoned Mine Land Grants..54
Federal Land Acquisition...55
Heritage Partnership Program...56
National Wildlife Refuge Fund..57

Department of Justice

Federal Prison System, Construction..58
State Criminal Alien Assistance Program...59

Department of Labor

Bureau of International Labor Affairs...60
Migrant and Seasonal Farmworker Training..61
Office of Disability Employment Policy...62
OSHA Training Grants..64
Senior Community Service Employment Program...65
WIOA Titles I and III Formula Programs (Adult, Youth, Dislocated Workers, Employment Service).66

Department of State and U.S. Agency for International Development

Development Assistance..67
Earmarked Appropriations for Non-Profit Organizations..68
Educational and Cultural Exchanges..69
Global Health Programs..70
International Organization Contributions..71
Overseas Contingency Operations..72
P.L. 480 Title II Food Aid..73
Peacekeeping..74

Departments of State/USAID and Treasury

Green Climate Fund and Global Climate Change Initiative..75

Department of Transportation

Capital Investment Grants (New Starts)..76
Essential Air Service...77
Grants to Amtrak...78

National Infrastructure Investments (TIGER)..79

Department of the Treasury

Community Development Financial Institutions Fund..80

Global Agriculture and Food Security Program..81

Special Inspector General for the Troubled Asset Relief Program...82

Corps of Engineers

Corps of Engineers - Agency Topline...83

Environmental Protection Agency

Categorical Grants..84

Energy Star and Voluntary Climate Programs...85

Enforcement...86

Geographic Programs...87

Research and Development..88

Superfund...89

National Aeronautics and Space Administration

Five Earth Science Missions..90

Office of Education..91

National Science Foundation

National Science Foundation, Research and Related Activities and Education Grants.........92

Other Independent Agencies

Chemical Safety Board...93

Corporation for National and Community Service..94

Corporation for Public Broadcasting..95

Institute of Museum and Library Services..96

International Development Foundations..97

Legal Services Corporation..98

National Endowment for the Arts..99

National Endowment for the Humanities...100

Neighborhood Reinvestment Corporation...101

Overseas Private Investment Corporation..102

Regional Commissions..103

U.S Institute of Peace..104
U.S. Trade and Development Agency..105
Woodrow Wilson International Center for Scholars..106

Mandatory Reforms

Multi-Agency

Eliminate Allocations to the Housing Trust Fund and Capital Magnet Fund....................107
Reduce Improper Payments and Other Program Integrity...108
Reform Federal Disability Programs 110
Reform Financial Regulation and Prevent Taxpayer-funded Bailouts................................113
Reform the Medical Liability System..114
Repeal and Replace Obamacare...115
Spectrum Auctions..116

Department of Agriculture

Agricultural Marketing Service User Fee..117
Animal and Plant Health Inspection Service User Fee...118
Eliminate Interest Payments to Electric and Telecommunications Utilities......................119
Eliminate the Rural Economic Development Program..120
Farm Bill Savings..121
Food Safety and Inspection Service User Fee...123
Grain Inspection, Packers and Stockyards Administration User Fee................................124
SNAP Reforms..125
SNAP Retailer Application Fee...126

Department of Education

Create Single Income-Driven Repayment Plan..127
Eliminate Account Maintenance Fee Payments to Guaranty Agencies.............................128
Eliminate Public Service Loan Forgiveness..129
Eliminate Subsidized Loans...130

Department of Energy

Power Marketing Administration Transmission Asset Divestiture....................................131
Repeal Borrowing Authority for Western Area Power Administration.............................132
Strategic Petroleum Reserve - Reduce by Half...133

Department of Health and Human Services

Eliminate the Social Services Block Grant..134

Reform Medicaid..135

Strengthen the Child Support Enforcement Program...136

Temporary Assistance for Needy Families Reforms...137

Department of Homeland Security

Extend Expiring Customs and Border Protection Fees..138

Reform of the National Flood Insurance Program..139

Department of the Interior

Cancel Southern Nevada Public Lands Management Act Balances...140

Federal Land Transaction Act Reauthorization..141

Gulf of Mexico Energy Security Act Repeal..142

Lease Oil and Gas in Arctic National Wildlife Refuge..143

Repeal Enhanced Geothermal Payments to Counties..144

Department of Labor

Pension Benefit Guaranty Corporation Multiemployer Premiums..145

Unemployment Insurance Solvency Standard..146

Department of the Treasury

Authority for Bureau of Engraving and Printing to Construct A New Facility.........................147

Require SSN for Child Tax Credit & Earned Income Tax Credit...148

Department of Veterans Affairs

Cap GI Bill Flight Training..149

Cost of Living Adjustments Round Down...150

Individual Unemployability...151

Corps of Engineers

Reform Inland Waterways Financing..152

Washington Aqueduct Divestiture...153

Office of Personnel Management

Increase Employee Contributions...154

Reduce Federal Retirement Benefits...155

Other Independent Agencies

Eliminate the Securities and Exchange Commission's Reserve Fund..156
Reform the Postal Service..157
Restructure the Consumer Financial Protection Bureau..158
Spectrum License Fee...159

MAJOR SAVINGS AND REFORMS IN THE PRESIDENT'S 2018 BUDGET

This volume describes major savings and reform proposals included in the 2018 President's Budget. It includes both discretionary and mandatory savings proposals that bring Federal spending under control and return the Federal budget to balance within 10 years. These proposals encompass a common sense approach to redefine the proper role of the Federal Government, and curtail programs that fall short on results or provide little return to the American people.

In total, this volume highlights 2018 savings of $57.3 billion in discretionary programs, including $26.7 billion in program eliminations and $30.6 billion in reductions. The volume also describes the major mandatory proposals summarized in Table S–6 of the *Budget* volume.

Going forward, the Administration will build on these proposals in order to implement the President's charge to create a leaner, more accountable, less intrusive, and more effective Government.

MAJOR DISCRETIONARY ELIMINATIONS
(Budget Authority in Millions)

	2017 CR	2018 Request	2018 Change from 2017
Agriculture			
McGovern-Dole International Food for Education	201	....	−201
Rural Business and Cooperative Service	95	....	−95
Rural Water and Waste Disposal Program Account	498	....	−498
Single Family Housing Direct Loans	61	....	−61
Total, Agriculture	**855**	....	**−855**
Commerce			
Economic Development Administration	251	30	−221
Manufacturing Extension Partnership	130	6	−124
Minority Business Development Agency	32	6	−26
National Oceanic and Atmospheric Administration Grants and Education	262	....	−262
Total, Commerce	**675**	**42**	**−633**
Education			
21st Century Community Learning Centers	1,164	....	−1,164
Comprehensive Literacy Development Grants	190	....	−190
Federal Supplemental Educational Opportunity Grants	732	....	−732
Impact Aid Payments for Federal Property	67	....	−67
International Education	72	....	−72
Strengthening Institutions	86	....	−86
Student Support and Academic Enrichment Grants	277	....	−277
Supporting Effective Instruction State Grants	2,345	....	−2,345
Teacher Quality Partnership	43	....	−43
Total, Education	**4,976**	....	**−4,976**
Energy			
Advanced Research Projects Agency—Energy	290	−26	−316
Advanced Technology Vehicle Manufacturing Loan Program and Title 17 Innovative Technology Loan Guarantee Program	21	....	−21
Mixed Oxide Fuel Fabrication Facility	340	279	−61
Total, Energy	**651**	**253**	**−398**
Health and Human Services			
Agency for Healthcare Research and Quality [1]	333	....	−333
Community Services Block Grant	714	....	−714
Health Professions and Nursing Training Programs	491	88	−403
Low Income Home Energy Assistance Program	3,384	....	−3,384
Total, Health and Human Services	**4,922**	**88**	**−4,834**
Homeland Security			
Flood Hazard Mapping and Risk Analysis Program	190	....	−190
Transportation Security Administration Law Enforcement Grants	45	....	−45
Total, Homeland	**235**	....	**−235**
Housing and Urban Development			
Choice Neighborhoods	125	....	−125
Community Development Block Grant	2,994	....	−2,994
HOME Investment Partnerships Program	948	....	−948
Self-Help and Assisted Homeownership Opportunity Program Account	56	....	−56
Total, Housing and Urban Development	**4,123**	....	**−4,123**
Interior			
Abandoned Mine Land Grants	90	....	−90
Heritage Partnership Program	20	1	−19
National Wildlife Refuge Fund	13	....	−13
Total, Interior	**123**	**1**	**−122**
Justice			
State Criminal Alien Assistance Program	210	....	−210
Total, Justice	**210**	....	**−210**

MAJOR DISCRETIONARY ELIMINATIONS—Continued
(Budget Authority in Millions)

	2017 CR	2018 Request	2018 Change from 2017
Labor			
Migrant and Seasonal Farmworker Training	82	....	−82
OSHA Training Grants	11	....	−11
Senior Community Service Employment Program	434	....	−434
Total, Labor	527	....	−527
State and USAID			
Development Assistance	2,509	....	−2,509
Earmarked Appropriations for Non-Profit Organizations			
The Asia Foundation	17	....	−17
East-West Center	17	....	−17
P.L. 480 Title II Food Aid	1,713	....	−1,713
Total, State and USAID	4,256	....	−4,256
State, USAID, and Treasury			
Green Climate Fund and Global Climate Change Initiative	1,590	....	−1,590
Total, State, USAID, and Treasury	1,590	....	−1,590
Transportation			
National Infrastructure Investments (TIGER)	499	....	−499
Total, Transportation	499	....	−499
Treasury			
Global Agriculture and Food Security Program	43	....	−43
Total, Treasury	43	....	−43
Environmental Protection Agency			
Energy Star and Voluntary Climate Programs	66	....	−66
Geographic Programs	427	....	−427
Total, Environmental Protection Agency	493	....	−493
National Aeronautics and Space Administration			
Five Earth Science Missions	191	....	−191
Office of Education	115	37	−78
Total, National Aeronautics and Space Administration	306	37	−269
Other Independent Agencies			
Chemical Safety Board	11	9	−2
Corporation for National and Community Service	1,093	135	−958
Corporation for Public Broadcasting	484	30	−454
Institute of Museum and Library Services	230	23	−207
International Development Foundations			
African Development Foundation	30	8	−22
Inter-American Foundation	22	5	−17
Legal Services Corporation	384	33	−351
National Endowment for the Arts	148	29	−119
National Endowment for the Humanities	148	42	−106
Neighborhood Reinvestment Corporation	175	27	−148
Overseas Private Investment Corporation	83	61	−22
Regional Commissions			
Appalachian Regional Commission	146	27	−119
Delta Regional Authority	25	3	−22
Denali Commission	15	7	−8
Northern Border Regional Commission	8	1	−7
U.S Institute of Peace	35	19	−16
U.S. Trade and Development Agency	60	12	−48
Woodrow Wilson International Center for Scholars	11	7	−4
Total, Other Independent Agencies	3,108	478	−2,630
Total Major Discretionary Eliminations	27,592	899	−26,693

[1] The 2018 Request includes $272 million within NIH to consolidate AHRQ's activities within NIH.

MAJOR DISCRETIONARY REDUCTIONS
(Budget Authority in Millions)

	2017 CR	2018 Request	2018 Change from 2017
Agriculture			
Conservation Operations	849	766	−83
Forest Service Land Acquisition	63	8	−55
Rural Development Salaries and Expenses	677	624	−53
Total, Agriculture	**1,589**	**1,398**	**−191**
Defense			
Base Realignment and Closure	....	....	....
Total, Defense	....	....	....
Education			
Federal Work Study	988	500	−488
Gaining Early Awareness for Undergraduate Programs	322	219	−103
TRIO	898	808	−90
Total, Education	**2,208**	**1,527**	**−681**
Energy			
Applied Energy Programs	3,760	1,606	−2,154
Total, Energy	**3,760**	**1,606**	**−2,154**
Health and Human Services			
Food and Drug Administration Medical Product User Fees	769	....	−769
National Institute for Occupational Safety and Health	338	200	−138
National Institutes of Health Topline	31,674	25,883	−5,791
Office of the National Coordinator for Health Information Technology	60	38	−22
Total, Health and Human Services	**32,841**	**26,121**	**−6,720**
Homeland Security			
Federal Emergency Management Agency State and Local Grants	1,979	1,212	−767
Total, Homeland	**1,979**	**1,212**	**−767**
Housing and Urban Development			
Grants to Native American Tribes and Alaska Native Villages	708	600	−108
Rental Assistance Programs	37,162	35,228	−1,934
Total, Housing and Urban Development	**37,870**	**35,828**	**−2,042**
Interior			
Federal Land Acquisition	183	54	−129
Total, Interior	**183**	**54**	**−129**
Justice			
Federal Prison System, Construction	444	−444	−888
Total, Justice	**444**	**−444**	**−888**
Labor			
Bureau of International Labor Affairs	86	19	−67
Office of Disability Employment Policy	38	27	−11
WIOA Titles I and III Formula Programs (Adult, Youth, Dislocated Workers, Employment Service)	3,474	2,133	−1,341
Total, Labor	**3,598**	**2,179**	**−1,419**
State and USAID			
Educational and Cultural Exchanges	590	285	−305
Global Health Programs	8,487	6,481	−2,006
International Organization Contributions	1,680	900	−780
Overseas Contingency Operations	19,195	12,017	−7,178
Peacekeeping	796	391	−405
Total, State and USAID	**30,748**	**20,074**	**−10,674**

MAJOR DISCRETIONARY REDUCTIONS—Continued
(Budget Authority in Millions)

	2017 CR	2018 Request	2018 Change from 2017
Transportation			
Capital Investment Grants (New Starts)	2,160	1,232	−928
Essential Air Service	175	....	−175
Grants to Amtrak	1,404	774	−630
Total, Transportation	**3,739**	**2,006**	**−1,733**
Treasury			
Community Development Financial Institutions Fund	234	14	−220
Special Inspector General for Troubled Asset Relief Program	41	20	−21
Total, Treasury	**275**	**34**	**−241**
Army Corps of Engineers			
Corps of Engineers - Agency Topline	5,978	5,002	−976
Total, Army Corps of Engineers	**5,978**	**5,002**	**−976**
Environmental Protection Agency			
Categorical Grants	1,079	597	−482
Enforcement	548	419	−129
Research and Development	483	249	−234
Superfund	1,092	762	−330
Total, Environmental Protection Agency	**3,202**	**2,027**	**−1,175**
National Science Foundation			
National Science Foundation, Research and Related Activities and Education Grants	6,900	6,124	−776
Total, National Science Foundation	**6,900**	**6,124**	**−776**
Total Major Discretionary Reductions	**135,314**	**104,748**	**−30,566**

MANDATORY SAVINGS PROPOSALS
(Outlays and Receipts in Millions of Dollars)

	Five Year Savings 2018–2022	Ten-Year Savings 2018–2027
Multi-Agency		
Eliminate Allocations to the Housing Trust Fund and Capital Magnet Fund	–1,043	–2,846
Reduce Improper Payments Government-wide	–8,872	–139,210
Other Program Integrity Initiatives	–3,766	–9,324
Reform Federal Disability Programs	–8,839	–72,475
Reform Financial Regulation and Prevent Taxpayer-funded Bailouts	–13,100	–35,000
Reform the Medical Liability System	–11,339	–55,013
Repeal and Replace Obamacare	–15,000	–250,000
Spectrum Auctions	–600	–6,600
Agriculture		
Agricultural Marketing Service User Fee	–100	–200
Animal and Plant Health Inspection Service User Fee	–100	–200
Eliminate Interest Payments to Electric and Telecommunications Utilities	–685	–1,377
Eliminate the Rural Economic Development Program	–477	–477
Farm Bill Savings	–15,108	–38,046
Food Safety and Inspection Service User Fee	–2,640	–5,940
Grain Inspection, Packers and Stockyards Administration User Fee	–150	–300
SNAP Reforms	–64,312	–190,932
SNAP Retailer Application Fee	–1,205	–2,355
Education		
Create Single Income-Driven Repayment Plan	–25,306	–76,404
Eliminate Account Maintenance Fee Payments to Guaranty Agencies	–443	–443
Eliminate Public Service Loan Forgiveness	–10,213	–27,471
Eliminate Subsidized Loans	–14,297	–38,873
Energy		
Power Administration Transmission Assets	–3,582	–5,512
Repeal Borrowing Authority for Western Area Power Administration	–3,990	–4,425
Strategic Petroleum Reserve - Reduce by Half	–4,368	–16,586
Health and Human Services		
Eliminate the Social Services Block Grant	–8,085	–16,470
Reform Medicaid	–70,000	–610,000
Strengthen the Child Support Enforcement Program	–873	–1,541
Temporary Assistance for Needy Families Reforms	–10,455	–21,655
Homeland Security		
Extend Expiring Customs and Border Protection Fees	....	–8,074
Reform of the National Flood Insurance Program	–2,606	–8,890
Interior		
Cancel Southern Nevada Public Lands Management Act Balances	–230	–230
Federal Land Transaction Act Reauthorization	–35	–35
Gulf of Mexico Energy Security Act Repeal	–1,685	–3,560
Lease Oil and Gas in Arctic National Wildlife Refuge	–400	–1,800
Repeal Enhanced Geothermal Payments to Counties	–17	–37
Labor		
Pension Benefit Guaranty Corporation Multiemployer Premiums	–6,409	–20,863
Unemployment Insurance Solvency Standard	–5,220	–12,912
Treasury		
Authority for Bureau of Engraving and Printing to Construct A New Facility	–401	–708
Require SSN for Child Tax Credit & Earned Income Tax Credit	–18,075	–40,411
Veterans Affairs		
Cap GI Bill Flight Training	–229	–511
Cost of Living Adjustments Round Down	–630	–2,677
Individual Unemployability	–17,922	–40,822

MANDATORY SAVINGS PROPOSALS—Continued
(Outlays and Receipts in Millions of Dollars)

	Five Year Savings 2018–2022	Ten-Year Savings 2018–2027
Corps of Engineers		
Reform Inland Waterways Financing	–530	–1,037
Washington Aqueduct Divestiture	–119	–119
Office of Personnel Management		
Increase Employee Contributions	–24,087	–72,055
Reduce Federal Retirement Benefits	–22,720	–76,845
Other Independent Agencies		
Eliminate the Securities and Exchange Commission's Reserve Fund	–200	–450
Reform the Postal Service	–22,077	–46,020
Restructure the Consumer Financial Protection Bureau	–2,910	–6,833
Spectrum License Fee	–1,450	–3,950

REDUCTION: CONSERVATION OPERATIONS
Department of Agriculture

The Budget proposes to reduce conservation operations by roughly 10 percent in an effort to encourage private sector participation in conservation planning.

Funding Summary
(In millions of dollars)

	2017 CR	2018 Request	2018 Change from 2017
Budget Authority	849	766	-83

Justification

Agricultural conservation planning is not an inherently governmental function. The private sector can provide this service, given uniform planning standards that are established by the Government. Currently the private sector offers planning assistance to farmers to implement precision pesticide and nutrient application, which is evidence that the private sector could also provide technical assistance for conservation planning. Farmers and other agricultural interest groups argue that the need for conservation planning is much greater than the funding resources currently available through the Government. When the Government funds technical assistance, it crowds out private sector competition. In the absence of Government funding, the private sector could increase farmers' access to technical assistance beyond what the Government currently offers.

REDUCTION: FOREST SERVICE LAND ACQUISITION
Department of Agriculture

The Budget proposes to reduce Federal land acquisition funding for the Forest Service to focus available funds on the protection and management of existing lands and assets.

Funding Summary
(In millions of dollars)

	2017 CR	2018 Request	2018 Change from 2017
Budget Authority	63	8	-55

Justification

The Budget for the Forest Service focuses limited resources on more effectively managing existing assets and lands. Land acquisition at the Forest Service is a lower priority than maintaining adequate funding for ongoing operations and maintenance of the National Forest System and for Wildland Fire Management programs. The Department of Agriculture's Forest Service already owns 193 million acres, mostly in the western United States. At a time when the Forest Service has billions of dollars in deferred maintenance, it needs to focus scarce resources and better manage what it owns before acquiring additional lands.

ELIMINATION: MCGOVERN-DOLE INTERNATIONAL FOOD FOR EDUCATION
Department of Agriculture

The Budget proposes to eliminate the McGovern-Dole International Food for Education program, which is duplicative of U.S. Agency for International Development (USAID) programs, lacks evidence that it is being effectively implemented, and has unaddressed oversight and performance monitoring challenges.

Funding Summary
(In millions of dollars)

	2017 CR	2018 Request	2018 Change from 2017
Budget Authority	201	0	-201

Justification

Research shows that school feeding programs in developing countries are usually high-cost investments with little to no returns, and are usually ineffective in achieving their goal to improve nutrition and learning outcomes, which are generally measured by weight and height gain and math performance and intelligence tests, respectively.[1] This is because, while these programs feed children, they have implementation challenges in developing countries and create a substitution effect, meaning children consume less at home once they receive a meal at school. In addition, during the 15-year operation of McGovern-Dole, auditors have found oversight weaknesses as reported by the Government Accountability Office (GAO), independent consultants, and the Department of Agriculture's (USDA) Office of Inspector General.[2] In the most recent GAO report in 2011, the GAO found weaknesses in performance monitoring, program evaluations, and prompt closeouts of agreements.[3] Weak performance monitoring cannot accurately show whether program objectives are achieved and ensure that sustainability is ultimately reached in the communities served once agreements close. While the GAO recommendations have technically been addressed, USDA is not able to provide evidence of substantive impacts on the nutrition of recipients. In addition, McGovern-Dole funding is duplicative of USAID which funds nutrition and education programs and the highest priority food aid programs.

Citations

[1] The United Nations University, Food and Nutrition Bulletin: *School feeding: Outcomes and Costs,* Vol.30 No. 2, (June 2009).

[2] Morgan Franklin Consulting: *Foreign Agricultural Service – Food for Progress and McGovern Dole Program Assessment,* (September 2013).

[3] Government Accountability Office: *International School Feeding: USDA's Oversight of the McGovern-Dole Food for Education Program Needs Improvement,* (May 2011).

ELIMINATION: RURAL BUSINESS AND COOPERATIVE SERVICE
Department of Agriculture

The Budget proposes to eliminate rural business and cooperative programs given findings that the programs have failed to meet the program goals and are improperly managed.

Funding Summary
(In millions of dollars)

	2017 CR	2018 Request	2018 Change from 2017
Budget Authority	95	0	-95

Justification

Year after year, the Government Accountability Office includes the Rural Business & Cooperative Service (RBS) in its annual report on fragmentation, overlap, and duplication, and the Department of Agriculture's (USDA) Inspector General found two of the Agency's largest loan and grant programs to be improperly managed.[1,2] RBS programs lack program evaluation, so it has not been possible to assess program impact. These programs have not been able to demonstrate that they meet the broader goals of reducing rural poverty, out-migration, or unemployment.

The Administration's tax, regulatory, and infrastructure policies are expected to be more effective at improving rural economies and job growth.

Citations

[1] United States Department of Agriculture, Office of Inspector General: *American Recovery and Reinvestment Act - Business and Industry Guaranteed Loans - Phase 3 Audit Report*, 34703-0001-32, (March 2013).

[2] United States Department of Agriculture, Office of Inspector General: *Rural Energy for America Program Audit Report*, 34001-0001-21, (August 2016).

REDUCTION: RURAL DEVELOPMENT SALARIES AND EXPENSES
Department of Agriculture

The Budget reduces funding for salaries and expenses in Rural Development (RD) due to the elimination of funding for the Rural Business Service programs, water and wastewater grants and loans, and single family housing direct loans. These major eliminations will reduce workload for the Rural Development Agencies, so less funding is needed.

Funding Summary
(In millions of dollars)

	2017 CR	2018 Request	2018 Change from 2017
Budget Authority	677	624	-53

Justification

The Budget reflects a realignment of RD's core operations and program delivery mechanisms to ensure that funding is delivered in the most cost effective way to rural communities, with a focus on achieving greater efficiency and eliminating potentially duplicative spending while supporting investments in infrastructure.

The primary priority will be to maintain the portfolio quality in loan making and servicing, and to protect the American public's interests in the loans outstanding. RD will also continue to have a local presence through its field offices. RD will examine the staffing distribution resulting from reductions and will look for efficiencies by coordinating with other Department of Agriculture agencies that are in shared locations with RD.

ELIMINATION: RURAL WATER AND WASTE DISPOSAL PROGRAM ACCOUNT
Department of Agriculture

The Budget proposes to eliminate the Department of Agriculture's (USDA) funding for water and wastewater treatment facilities because it duplicates the Environmental Protection Agency's (EPA) State Revolving funds (SRFs). The Administration believes that EPA or private sector sources should fund this activity.

Funding Summary
(In millions of dollars)

	2017 CR	2018 Request	2018 Change from 2017
Budget Authority	498	0	-498

Note: Loan Level provided in 2017 CR is $1.2 billion, and grants were approximately $480 million for a total program level of $1.7 billion.

Justification

Funding small, rural treatment facilities could be handled by EPA's SRFs. USDA's water and wastewater program was created years before any large national program was available to address community water treatment facilities. Currently, the key Federal program for water infrastructure financing is EPA's SRFs. Since their creation, the SRFs have been federally capitalized with more than $60 billion, and are a legitimate resource for financing rural water treatment facilities. Moreover, the absence of the USDA program might stimulate infrastructure lending from rural lenders as well as CoBank and the National Rural Utilities Cooperative Finance Corporation. CoBank has already committed $10 billion for this purpose through their involvement with the Rural Infrastructure Opportunity (ROI) Fund, which is a private sector investment initiative for financing infrastructure in rural America.

ELIMINATION: SINGLE FAMILY HOUSING DIRECT LOANS
Department of Agriculture

The Budget proposes to eliminate funding for the Department of Agriculture's (USDA) rural single family housing direct loan program. Beginning in 2018, USDA will offer home ownership assistance only through its single family housing guaranteed loans. Financial markets have become more efficient, and increased the reach of mortgage credit to lower credit qualities and incomes. Therefore, utilizing the private banking industry to provide this service, with a guarantee from the Federal Government, is a more efficient way to deliver this assistance.

Funding Summary
(In millions of dollars)

	2017 CR	2018 Request	2018 Change from 2017
Budget Authority	61	0	-61

[1] Loan Level provided in 2017 CR is approximately $1 billion.

Justification

Historically, USDA has offered both direct and guaranteed homeownership loans. The direction of Rural Development's single family housing mortgage assistance over the last two decades has been toward guaranteed loans. The single family housing guaranteed loan program was newly authorized in 1990 at $100 million and has grown to a $24 billion loan program annually. Meanwhile the single family direct loan program has been stagnant at approximately a $1 billion loan level.

Moreover, current historically low mortgage rates often result in an average 30-year fixed commercial mortgage rate at or below the average borrower rate for the USDA single family direct loan. Given that graduating to private credit is a goal of the direct program, pointing borrowers to commercial credit with a Federal guarantee is a preferred way to achieve the USDA policy goal of providing homeownership opportunities to low income rural residents.

Furthermore, rural areas once isolated from easy access to credit have shrunk as broadband internet access and correspondent lending have grown. Therefore, USDA is now in a position to utilize solely the guarantee program and still achieve the Administration's home ownership goals for rural areas at a lower cost to the taxpayers.

ELIMINATION: ECONOMIC DEVELOPMENT ADMINISTRATION
Department of Commerce

The Budget proposes to eliminate the Economic Development Administration (EDA) and provide $30 million to conduct an orderly closure beginning in 2018. EDA's grant programs are duplicative of other economic development programs within the Federal Government and State and local efforts.

Funding Summary
(In millions of dollars)

	2017 CR	2018 Request	2018 Change from 2017
Budget Authority	251	30	-221

Justification

The proposed elimination of EDA is a part of a broader effort to eliminate duplicative and unauthorized economic development programs across the Federal Government. The Congress has not authorized EDA's development assistance grants since the authority expired in 2008.[1] A 2011 Government Accountability Office (GAO) report found that each of the 80 economic development programs at the four departments it reviewed (Departments of Commerce, Housing and Urban Development, Agriculture, and the Small Business Administration) overlapped with at least one of the other programs reviewed.[2] A subsequent GAO report found that EDA's yet-to-be activated manufacturing loan guarantee program, "does not clearly differentiate its potential applicants from those of the comparable Federal loan guarantee programs GAO identified."[3]

Citations

[1] Congressional Budget Office: *Unauthorized Appropriations and Expiring Authorizations*, (January 2017).

[2] Government Accountability Office: *Efficiency and Effectiveness of Fragmented Economic Development Programs Are Unclear*, GAO-11-477R, (May 2011).

[3] Government Accountability Office: *Additional Opportunities to Reduce Fragmentation, Overlap, and Duplication and Achieve Other Financial Benefits*, GAO-16-375SP, (April 2016).

ELIMINATION: MANUFACTURING EXTENSION PARTNERSHIP
Department of Commerce

The Budget proposes to eliminate Federal funding for the Manufacturing Extension Partnership (MEP), saving $124 million after accounting for the cost of closing the program. The Administration is seeking to end funding for organizations that duplicate the efforts of other Federal programs or the non-profit and private sectors. In 2018 the National Institute of Standards and Technology will work to transition MEP centers solely to non-Federal revenue streams, as was intended when the program was first established.

Funding Summary
(In millions of dollars)

	2017 CR	2018 Request	2018 Change from 2017
Budget Authority	130	6	-124

Justification

The Federal MEP program subsidizes advisory and consulting services for small and medium-sized manufacturers through a network of state MEP centers. When the program began, Federal funding for a center was limited to no more than six years to stand up the center, after which the center was intended to transition to entirely non-Federal funding sources. However, many of these MEP centers have been receiving Federal funding for decades, and many of the services provided by MEP centers can be obtained elsewhere.

For many years critics have labeled the MEP program as "corporate welfare" since it provides direct support to industry,[1,2] and the Congressional Budget Office identified the program as suitable for elimination nearly a decade ago.[3]

Citations

[1] United States Senate Committee on Government Affairs: *The Advanced Technology Program and other Corporate Subsidies,* Statement of Stephen Moore, Director of Federal Policy, CATO Institute, (June 3, 1997).

[2] Republican Study Committee: *Fiscal Year 2017 Blueprint for a Balanced Budget 2.0.*

[3] Congressional Budget Office: *Budget Options: Volume 2,* (August 2009).

ELIMINATION: MINORITY BUSINESS DEVELOPMENT AGENCY
Department of Commerce

The Budget proposes to eliminate the Minority Business Development Agency (MBDA) and provide $6 million to close the agency beginning in 2018. MBDA provides minority business enterprises with a variety of business assistance services that are duplicative of other Federal, State, local, and private sector efforts.

Funding Summary
(In millions of dollars)

	2017 CR	2018 Request	2018 Change from 2017
Budget Authority	32	6	-26

Justification

The elimination of MBDA is part of a broader effort to eliminate duplicative and unauthorized economic development programs across the Federal Government. MBDA funds business centers through cooperative agreements with non-profit organizations that are duplicative of other Federal efforts, including Small Business Administration (SBA) District Offices and Small Business Development Centers, as well as State and local government centers providing certification and assistance to minority business entities. As opposed to SBA, MBDA attempts to focus on supporting "medium sized" businesses; however, these size standards are not defined on an industry-by-industry basis as they are for programs following SBA's small business size standards. Additionally, the economic impact of the MBDA business centers is difficult to quantify due to the small size of the cooperative agreements and the self-reporting metrics from the grant recipients.

ELIMINATION: NATIONAL OCEANIC AND ATMOSPHERIC ADMINISTRATION GRANTS AND EDUCATION

Department of Commerce

The Budget proposes to eliminate funding for several lower priority, and in many cases, unauthorized, National Oceanic and Atmospheric Administration (NOAA) grant and education programs, including Sea Grant, the National Estuarine Research Reserve System, Coastal Zone Management Grants, the Office of Education, and the Pacific Coastal Salmon Recovery Fund. These eliminations would allow NOAA to better target remaining resources to core missions and services.

Funding Summary
(In millions of dollars)

	2017 CR	2018 Request	2018 Change from 2017
Budget Authority	262	0	-262

Justification

These grant and education programs generally support State, local, and/or industry interests, and these entities may choose to continue some of this work with their own funding. In addition, these grants often are not optimally targeted, in many instances favoring certain species or geographic areas over others or distributing funds by formula rather than directing them to programs and projects with the greatest need or potential benefit. NOAA will continue to serve as a resource and provide technical assistance as appropriate on many of the issues funded by these programs.

REDUCTION: BASE REALIGNMENT AND CLOSURE
Department of Defense

The Department of Defense (DOD) has approximately 20 percent excess infrastructure capacity across all Military Departments. The best way to eliminate DOD's unneeded infrastructure is through the Base Realignment and Closure (BRAC) process. If the Congress authorizes DOD to begin a new round of BRAC in 2021, DOD estimates it could generate $2 billion or more in annual savings by 2027. These savings would be re-invested in higher priority DOD needs.

Justification

The 2018 Budget requests authorization to pursue a BRAC round beginning in 2021. DOD estimates that it has approximately 20 percent excess capacity spread across the Military Departments and projects it could save $2 billion or more annually by 2027. By executing BRAC in 2021, DOD will have the opportunity to reduce unnecessary infrastructure and align its facilities with the force structure determined by the National Defense Strategy. DOD has not conducted a BRAC round since 2005, but has sought BRAC authority and been denied by the Congress each year since 2013.

ELIMINATION: 21ST CENTURY COMMUNITY LEARNING CENTERS
Department of Education

The Budget proposes eliminating the 21st Century Community Learning Centers (21st CCLC) program given performance data demonstrates that the program is not achieving its goals, and the program has low participant attendance rates; nearly 60 percent of students attended a 21st CCLC center for 30 days or fewer during the 2014-2015 school year.

Funding Summary
(In millions of dollars)

	2017 CR	2018 Request	2018 Change from 2017
Budget Authority	1,164	0	-1,164

Justification

The 21st CCLC program enables communities to establish or expand centers that provide additional student learning opportunities through before- and after-school programs, and summer school programs, aimed at improving student academic outcomes. While limited evaluation and survey data from certain States and individual centers highlights benefits from participation, such as improved behavior and classroom grades, overall program performance data show that the 21st CCLC is not achieving its goal of helping students, particularly those who attend low-performing schools, meet challenging State academic standards. For example, on average from 2013 to 2015, less than 20 percent of program participants improved from not proficient to proficient or above on State assessments in reading and mathematics. Additionally, student improvement in academic grades was limited, with States reporting higher math and english grades for less than half of regular program participants. Low attendance rates at the program's centers likely are a key explanation for the program's limited impact on academic outcomes. For example, States reported that fewer than half of all students served (752,000 out of 1.8 million) attended programs for 30 days or more during the 2014-2015 school year. These recent results are consistent with findings of the last rigorous national evaluation of the program, conducted in 2005, which also found the program had limited academic impact and low student attendance rates.[1]

These data strongly suggest that the 21st CCLC is not generating the benefits commensurate with an annual investment of more than $1 billion in limited Federal education funds. Moreover, the provision of before- and after-school academic enrichment opportunities may be better supported with other Federal, State, local or private funds, including the $15 billion Title I Grants to Local Educational Agencies program.

Citations

[1] U.S. Department of Education, National Center for Education Evaluation and Regional Assistance: *When Schools Stay Open Late: The National Evaluation of the 21st Century Community Learning Centers Program: Final Report*, (October 2004).

ELIMINATION: COMPREHENSIVE LITERACY DEVELOPMENT GRANTS
Department of Education

The Budget proposes eliminating the Comprehensive Literacy Development Grants program (formerly known as Striving Readers), given the program has limited impact and duplicates activities that may be supported with other Federal, State, local, and private funds.

Funding Summary
(In millions of dollars)

	2017 CR	2018 Request	2018 Change from 2017
Budget Authority	190	0	-190

Justification

The Comprehensive Literacy Development Grants program makes competitive awards to States to improve literacy instruction from birth through grade 12. The program has limited impact and duplicates activities that may be supported by other sources of both Federal and non-Federal funds. For example, the Title I Grants to Local Educational Agencies program provides over $15 billion to more than 14,000 school districts that may be used to support effective, evidence-based reading instruction. By comparison, the last cohort of Striving Readers grants served only six States and just a handful of districts in each State. Moreover, a 2015 study by the Institute of Education Sciences indicated that a majority (six out of ten) of the interventions implemented by the 2009 and 2006 grant cohorts had no discernible effects on reading achievement.[1] States or school districts that want to test or expand the use of evidence-based literacy instruction may seek funding under the Education Innovation and Research program, which provides grant awards for scaling up effective practices that are comparable in size to those available through the Comprehensive Literacy Development Grants program.

Citations

[1] U.S. Department of Education, National Center for Education Evaluation and Regional Assistance, Institute of Education Sciences: *Summary of Research Generated by Striving Readers on the Effectiveness of Interventions for Struggling Adolescent Readers*, NCEE 2016-4001, (2015).

ELIMINATION: FEDERAL SUPPLEMENTAL EDUCATIONAL OPPORTUNITY GRANTS
Department of Education

The Budget proposes to eliminate the Federal Supplemental Educational Opportunity Grant (SEOG) program, given the program is a less targeted way to deliver need-based grant aid than Pell Grants. Eliminating the program would also reduce complexity in Federal student aid.

Funding Summary
(In millions of dollars)

	2017 CR	2018 Request	2018 Change from 2017
Budget Authority	732	0	-732

Justification

The SEOG program provides need-based grant aid to eligible undergraduate students to help reduce financial barriers to postsecondary education. Currently, SEOG awards are not optimally allocated based on a student's financial need, despite being a need-based program. Although participating institutions must give "priority" in awarding SEOG funds to Pell-eligible students, there is no requirement that the size of these awards be tied to the need of the student. As a result, institutions are given the discretion to provide larger SEOG awards to students that do not exhibit the highest need. In fact, Department of Education data show that the average SEOG award in award year 2014-2015 increased as student income levels increased. Furthermore, provisions in the SEOG funding allocation formula also distort the targeting of aid. For example, Department data show that about 67 percent of Pell funding goes to students attending public four-year or public two-year institutions, while only 50 percent of SEOG funds go to these institutions. Moreover, the SEOG program is part of a complex array of Federal aid programs that could benefit from better targeting of aid to needy students. In award year 2017-2018, the Department is expected to pay institutions over $14.5 million dollars to administer the SEOG program dollars that could be better targeted directly to needy students. This program's authorization expired in 2014.

REDUCTION: FEDERAL WORK STUDY
Department of Education

The Budget proposes to significantly reduce Federal funds for the Federal Work-Study (FWS) program beginning in award year 2018-2019 while also improving the targeting of aid by limiting eligibility to undergraduate students who can most benefit.

Funding Summary
(In millions of dollars)

	2017 CR	2018 Request	2018 Change from 2017
Budget Authority	988	500	-488

Justification

The FWS program assists needy undergraduate and graduate students in financing postsecondary education costs through part-time employment. However, the program includes outdated provisions in allocating funding and in determining student need that make it inefficient at allocating funds to the neediest students.

The Budget would ensure that institutions prioritize eligible Pell Grant recipients when allocating FWS program funds. According to Department data, among dependent students, those with family incomes at or above $30,000 received 66 percent of FWS funds compared to 33 percent of FWS funds going to students with family incomes below $30,000. Independent students, who typically have lower family incomes, received nearly half of all Pell Grant aid, but only received 14 percent of FWS funds. This program's authorization expired in 2014.

REDUCTION: GAINING EARLY AWARENESS FOR UNDERGRADUATE PROGRAMS
Department of Education

The Budget proposes reducing Gaining Early Awareness for Undergraduate Programs (GEAR UP). Many of the services provided by GEAR UP are duplicative of other Department of Education programs, such as Talent Search (one of the five TRIO programs), and there is limited evidence that GEAR UP is effective at increasing college access and persistence of its participants.

Funding Summary
(In millions of dollars)

	2017 CR	2018 Request	2018 Change from 2017
Budget Authority	322	219	-103

Justification

GEAR UP provides grants to States to support college preparation and awareness activities to ensure low-income elementary, middle, and secondary students are prepared for and enroll in postsecondary education. The 2018 request would allow existing grantees to provide a continuity of service, but the Department would not make any additional awards in 2018 pending the outcome of a rigorous evaluation of a promising advising strategy used in the program. Many of the activities supported under GEAR UP can be supported through the Federal TRIO Programs and ESEA Title I grants to States. In addition, there is limited rigorous evidence that the program is effective, particularly in increasing high school graduation and college enrollment rates. Although a 2008 evaluation found a positive association between GEAR UP participation and some early outcomes such as increasing students' and parents' knowledge of postsecondary opportunities and increasing rigorous course-taking, there was no indication of an association with improved grades or school behavior.[1] GEAR UP grantees are, however, participating in a rigorous, Department-funded evaluation of an advising strategy that has the potential to improve students' initial enrollment and persistence in college.

Citations

[1] U.S. Department of Education, Office of Planning, Evaluation, and Policy Development, Policy and Program Studies Service: *Early Outcomes of the GEAR UP Program: Final Report,* (2008).

ELIMINATION: IMPACT AID PAYMENTS FOR FEDERAL PROPERTY
Department of Education

The Budget proposes eliminating Impact Aid Payments for Federal Property. These payments compensate school districts for the presence of Federal property without regard for the presence of federally-connected students, and therefore do not necessarily support the education of federally-connected students, which is the intent of the Impact Aid program.

Funding Summary
(In millions of dollars)

	2017 CR	2018 Request	2018 Change from 2017
Budget Authority	67	0	-67

Justification

The primary purpose of the Impact Aid program is to help pay for the education of federally-connected children, and fund programs that serve federally-connected children. The Payments for Federal Property program compensates school districts for lost property tax revenue due to the presence of Federal lands without regard to whether those districts educate any federally-connected children as a result of the Federal presence. When this authority was established in 1950, its purpose was to provide assistance to local educational agencies (LEAs) in cases where the Federal Government had imposed a substantial and continuing burden by acquiring a considerable portion of real property in the LEA. The law applied only to property acquired since 1938 because, in general, LEAs had been able to adjust to acquisitions that occurred before that time. The Administration believes that the majority of LEAs receiving assistance under this program have now had sufficient time to adjust to the removal of the property from their tax rolls.

ELIMINATION: INTERNATIONAL EDUCATION
Department of Education

The Budget eliminates the International Education and Foreign Language Studies Domestic and Overseas Programs, which are designed to strengthen the capability and performance of American education in foreign languages and international studies. Other Federal Agencies whose primary mission is national security implement similar programs and are better equipped to support the objective of these programs.

Funding Summary
(In millions of dollars)

	2017 CR	2018 Request	2018 Change from 2017
Budget Authority	72	0	-72

Justification

While the Administration recognizes the critical need for our Nation to have a readily available pool of international, regional, and advanced language experts for economic, foreign affairs, and national security purposes, it is unclear that this goal is consistent with the Department of Education's core mission. Other Federal agencies, whose primary mission is national security, implement similar programs and are better equipped to support this critical objective. Therefore, the Budget proposes to eliminate these duplicative programs. The authorization for these programs expired in 2014.

ELIMINATION: STRENGTHENING INSTITUTIONS
Department of Education

The Budget does not include funding for the Strengthening Institutions Program (SIP). SIP is duplicative of other Title III and V program funding for institutional support activities. The Budget preserves funding for Title III and V programs that support Historically Black Colleges and Universities (HBCUs) and Minority-Serving Institutions (MSIs), consistent with the President's executive order on HBCUs.

Funding Summary
(In millions of dollars)

	2017 CR	2018 Request	2018 Change from 2017
Budget Authority	86	0	-86

Justification

All of the institutional support activities authorized under the Strengthening Institutions Program are also authorized under other Title III and V programs that provide discretionary and mandatory funding for a wide range of authorized institutional support activities including strengthening infrastructure and enhancing fiscal stability. Strengthening the quality of educational opportunities in institutions of higher education dedicated to serving low-income and minority students is a critical part of the Administration's efforts to foster more and better opportunities in higher education for communities that are often underserved, as the President asserted in his recent executive order on HBCUs. Accordingly, the Budget protects funding for Title III and V programs that support HBCUs and MSIs that specifically serve large numbers of minority students.

SIP as well as other Title III and V programs are authorized by the Higher Education Act (HEA), which has not been reauthorized since the 2008 Higher Education Opportunity Act. Authorization of the HEA technically expired in 2014.

ELIMINATION: STUDENT SUPPORT AND ACADEMIC ENRICHMENT GRANTS
Department of Education

The Budget proposes eliminating the Student Support and Academic Enrichment Grants program. The Administration does not believe limited Federal resources should be allocated to this program given that the program allows the funds to be distributed to all school districts that receive Title I, Part A funds, which makes it likely that award amounts will be too small to have a meaningful impact. The funding is also duplicative of other Federal and non-Federal funding, including the $15 billion Title I Grants to Local Educational Agencies program.

Funding Summary
(In millions of dollars)

	2017 CR	2018 Request	2018 Change from 2017
Budget Authority	277	0	-277

Note: 2017 CR level includes funding for the four programs that were consolidated.

Justification

The Student Support and Academic Enrichment Grants program, newly authorized under the Every Student Succeeds Act of 2015, consolidated four previously authorized programs: Mathematics and Science Partnerships, Advanced Placement, Elementary and Secondary School Counseling, and Physical Education. The Program provides funding to school districts for activities that support well-rounded educational opportunities (e.g. arts, STEM), safe and healthy students, and the effective use of technology. Subgrants can be awarded by formula to all school districts that receive Title I, Part A funds, which at the current funding level of $400 million, would result in award amounts of less than $30,000 for the vast majority of school districts. The Administration does not believe limited Federal resources should be allocated to a program where many of its grants will likely be too small to have a meaningful impact. Furthermore, the school districts that do receive at least $30,000 must follow funding restrictions that prescribe a minimum amount that must be spent on the program's different categories of activities, further diluting the program's impact and removing discretion that is best left to local decision-makers. Also, the activities authorized under this program generally can be supported with funds from other Federal, State, local, and private sources, including similarly flexible funds provided under the $15 billion Title I Grants to LEAs program.

ELIMINATION: SUPPORTING EFFECTIVE INSTRUCTION STATE GRANTS
Department of Education

The Budget proposes eliminating Supporting Effective Instruction (SEI) State Grants (Title II State grants), a program that provides formula funds to States to improve the quality and effectiveness of teachers, principals, and other schools leaders. SEI grants are poorly targeted and funds are spread too thinly to have a meaningful impact on student outcomes. In addition, there is limited evidence that teacher professional development, a primary activity funded by the program, has led to increases in student achievement.

Funding Summary
(In millions of dollars)

	2017 CR	2018 Request	2018 Change from 2017
Budget Authority	2,345	0	-2,345

Justification

The Budget proposes eliminating Supporting Effective Instruction (SEI) State Grants program. While the SEI State Grants program authorizes a wide range of activities, in school year 2015-2016, 52 percent of funds were used for professional development (PD) and 25 percent were used for class-size reduction. An LEA that identifies either activity as a key strategy for responding to a comprehensive needs assessment may use Title I, Part A funds for the same purpose. Title I funds also may be used to recruit and retain effective teachers. In addition, professional development, as currently provided, has shown limited impact on student achievement. For example, a recent evaluation of an intensive elementary school mathematics PD program found that while the PD improved teacher knowledge and led to improvements in teachers' use and quality of explanation in the classroom, there was no difference in student achievement test scores on either the State assessment or on a study-administered math test.[1] Additional Department of Education-funded studies of PD have found similar results.[2,3] While class size reduction has been shown to increase student achievement, school districts used SEI State grant funds to pay the salaries of an estimated 8,000 teachers in school year 2015-2016, out of a total nationwide teacher workforce of roughly three million teachers. These data suggest that eliminating the program is likely to have minimal impact on class sizes or teacher staffing levels.

Citations

[1] Institute of Education Sciences: *Middle School Mathematics Professional Development Impact Study*, (May 2011).

[2] Institute of Education Sciences: *Elementary School Reading Professional Development Impact Evaluation*, (September 2008).

[3] Institute of Education Sciences: *Does Content-focused Teacher Professional Development Work? Findings from Three Institute of Education Sciences Studies*, (November 2016).

ELIMINATION: TEACHER QUALITY PARTNERSHIP
Department of Education

The Budget proposes eliminating the Teacher Quality Partnerships (TPQ) program. There is limited evidence that the program is any more effective than other State- and locally-driven initiatives designed to train and retain highly effective teachers in critical shortage areas.

Funding Summary
(In millions of dollars)

	2017 CR	2018 Request	2018 Change from 2017
Budget Authority	43	0	-43

Justification

The TQP program supports partnerships to create a variety of effective pathways into teaching and increase the number of teachers effective in improving student outcomes. The TQP authority is overly restrictive and does not provide States, school districts, and institutions of higher education sufficient flexibilities to meaningfully design systems of teacher preparation, recruitment, and induction that meet their staffing needs. In addition, funding to support partnerships that enhance professional development activities and training for current and prospective teachers and staff may be provided through Elementary and Secondary Education Act formula grant funds (e.g., Title I), as well as from competitive grant programs. There is also limited evidence that demonstrates this program is any more effective than other State- and locally-driven initiatives designed to train and retain highly effective teachers in critical shortage areas.

REDUCTION: TRIO
Department of Education

The Budget proposes reducing Federal TRIO Programs. The Budget maintains funding for the original three TRIO programs while eliminating funding for two TRIO programs, which are duplicative and have limited evidence of increasing college access or completion.

Funding Summary
(In millions of dollars)

	2017 CR	2018 Request	2018 Change from 2017
Budget Authority	898	808	-90

Justification

Federal TRIO programs consist of five programs that support services to encourage individuals from disadvantaged backgrounds to enter and complete postsecondary education. The Budget request maintains support for the original three TRIO programs (Upward Bound (UB), Talent Search (TS), and Student Support Services (SSS)), but eliminates support for the McNair Post-baccalaureate Achievement (McNair) and Educational Opportunity Centers (EOC) programs. The Budget supports the Administration's prioritization for TRIO programs that: 1) assist middle school, high school, and college students in moving through the academic pipeline through college completion; and 2) have shown some evidence of effectiveness or are designed to support strategies in areas where there is a growing body of evidence. The evidence of effectiveness varies across TRIO programs. For example, a 2009 evaluation of UB found positive impacts of the program for key subgroups[1] - including students in rural areas and students who did not expect to earn a bachelor's degree. Further, there is a growing body of evidence suggesting the effectiveness of specific strategies that can be used in TS, UB, UBMS, and SSS to improve college access and completion for disadvantaged students. Conversely, there is limited evidence of effectiveness for both the McNair and EOC programs. While the goals of McNair and EOC programs are important, McNair is a high cost program that serves relatively few students and EOC offers "low touch" services that can be provided through other programs like TS and Adult Education State Grants. Colleges and universities can also use institutional resources to support the same objectives included under these two programs. Furthermore, a 2008 Department of Education analysis released found that only six percent of McNair participants served between 1989 and 1998 had earned doctorates by 2003.[2]

Citations

[1] U.S. Department of Education, Office of Planning, Evaluation, and Policy Development, Policy and Program Studies Service: *The Impacts of Regular Upward-Bound on Postsecondary Outcomes 7-9 Years After Scheduled High School Graduation: Final Report*, (2009).

[2] U.S. Department of Education, Office of Planning, Evaluation, and Policy Development, Policy and Program Studies Service: *The Educational and Employment Outcomes of the Ronald E. McNair Postbaccalaureate Achievement Program Alumni*, (2008).

ELIMINATION: ADVANCED RESEARCH PROJECTS AGENCY - ENERGY
Department of Energy

The Budget proposes to eliminate the Advanced Research Project Agency-Energy (ARPA-E) program because the private sector is better positioned to finance disruptive energy technology research and development.

Funding Summary
(In millions of dollars)

	2017 CR	2018 Request	2018 Change from 2017
Budget Authority	290	-26	-316

Note: This account includes a $20 million appropriation and a $46 million cancellation for net budget authority of -$26 million.

Justification

ARPA-E is a separate office within the Department of Energy (DOE) that supports energy projects. Appropriations for ARPA-E were only authorized through 2013 under the America COMPETES Reauthorization Act of 2010 (P.L. 111-358). In addition, there has been concern about the potential for ARPA-E's efforts to overlap with Research & Development (R&D) being carried out, or which should be carried out, by the private sector. The Budget includes $20 million for program closeout activities, which will be supplemented by the use of $45 million in prior year, unobligated balances to ensure full closure of ARPA-E by mid-2019. Any remaining contract closeout and award monitoring activities will be transferred elsewhere within DOE. A shutdown plan would be developed in FY 2018 to ensure prudent monitoring and management of ARPA-E contracts and responsible stewardship of taxpayer funds continues after the ARPA-E office closes. This proposed elimination reflects both a streamlining of Federal activities and a refocusing on the proper Federal role in energy R&D.

ELIMINATION: ADVANCED TECHNOLOGY VEHICLE MANUFACTURING LOAN PROGRAM AND TITLE 17 INNOVATIVE TECHNOLOGY LOAN GUARANTEE PROGRAM
Department of Energy

The Budget proposes to eliminate the Title XVII Innovative Technology Loan Guarantee Program and the Advanced Technology Vehicle Manufacturing Loan Program because the private sector is better positioned to finance innovative technologies. The Loan Programs Office would continue to conduct monitoring of existing loans.

Funding Summary
(In millions of dollars)

	2017 CR	2018 Request	2018 Change from 2017
Budget Authority	21	0	-21

Note: In addition to eliminating program management funding, the Budget also proposes to cancel $383 million in unobligated balances from Title XVII and $4.3 billion from ATVM. There are no scoreable savings for these cancellations.

Justification

The relative inactivity of these programs indicates they are ineffective at attracting borrowers with viable projects who are unable to secure private sector financing and supports the position that financing innovative energy and advanced vehicle manufacturing projects is a more appropriate role for the private sector. In addition, authority for loans made under the Recovery Act has expired. Specifically:

Innovative Technologies. Only three loan guarantees have been closed through this program since its inception, all related to a single project totaling approximately $8 billion. Efforts to increase the attractiveness of the program to potential borrowers have not yielded increased loan activity. The Budget proposes to cancel all remaining loan volume authority. In addition, the Budget proposes to permanently cancel unobligated balances that were appropriated under the American Reinvestment and Recovery Act of 2009 (Public Law 111-5). That Act provided $2.5 billion in credit subsidy for a temporary program to support loan guarantees. This authority has expired, and the unobligated balances are not currently available for new loans. The Budget proposes to cancel $383 million in unobligated credit subsidy while retaining $96 million already set aside to cover the cost of potential modifications.

Advance Technology Vehicles. Since its inception in 2007 only five loans have been closed under this authority and since 2011, no new loans have closed. Efforts to increase the attractiveness of the program to potential borrowers have not yielded increased loan activity. The Budget proposes to cancel all remaining loan volume authority and appropriated credit subsidy.

REDUCTION: APPLIED ENERGY PROGRAMS
Department of Energy

The Budget proposes to reduce funding for the Department of Energy's (DOE) four applied energy research and development (R&D) program areas: Energy Efficiency and Renewable Energy, Fossil Energy, Nuclear Energy, and Electricity Delivery and Energy Reliability. The proposal focuses Federal activities on early-stage R&D and reflects an increased reliance on the private sector to fund later-stage R&D, including demonstration, commercialization, and deployment where the private sector has a clear incentive to invest.

Funding Summary
(In millions of dollars)

	2017 CR	2018 Request	2018 Change from 2017
Non-Defense Budget Authority	3,760	1,606	-2,154

Justification

The private sector is best positioned and motivated to evaluate the commercial potential of emerging energy technologies and technology advancements relative to the risks of R&D investment. Private sector-led R&D tends to focus on near-term cost and performance improvements where the certainty of profit generation or the prospect of successful market entry are greatest. The Federal role in energy R&D is strongest at the earlier stages, where the greatest motivation is the generation of new knowledge and the proving of novel concepts. In recent years, the applied energy R&D programs have tilted heavily toward subsidizing the later stage development, demonstration, and deployment of new energy technologies. The Budget refocuses these programs on energy challenges which present a significant degree of scientific or technical uncertainty across a relatively lengthy time span, making it unlikely that industry will invest significant R&D on their own. In addition, the DOE-funded applied energy National Laboratories will remain open and operational, while refocusing efforts on early-stage R&D.

Within these reductions, the Budget eliminates the Weatherization Assistance Program and State Energy Program. This reduces Federal intervention in State-level energy policy and implementation and focuses funding for the Office of Energy Efficiency and Renewable Energy on limited, early-stage applied energy research and development.

ELIMINATION: MIXED OXIDE FUEL FABRICATION FACILITY TERMINATION
Department of Energy

The Budget proposes to terminate the Mixed Oxide (MOX) Fuel Fabrication Facility (MFFF) project and to pursue an alternative disposition method that will achieve significant long-term savings.

Funding Summary
(In millions of dollars)

	2017 CR	2018 Request	2018 Change from 2017
MFFF Construction	340	0	-340
MFFF Termination	0	270	270
Dilute and Dispose Strategy	0	9	9

Justification

The United States began construction of the MFFF in 2007 in accord with the Plutonium Management and Disposition Agreement (PMDA) between the United States and Russia. However, due to the project's 350-percent cost growth and a 32-year schedule slip, both the Department of Energy and external independent analyses have consistently concluded that the MOX approach to plutonium disposition is significantly costlier and would require a much higher annual budget than an alternate disposition method, Dilute and Dispose (D&D). The termination of the MFFF project and pursuit of D&D presents a significant long-term cost savings and is projected to take less time to dispose of the plutonium covered under the PMDA. The D&D strategy will disposition surplus U.S. weapon-grade plutonium by diluting with an inert agent and disposing of it at a geologic repository.

The goal of the Nonproliferation Construction program is to build facilities to dispose of at least 34 metric tons of surplus U.S. weapon-grade plutonium by fabricating it into MOX fuel and irradiating it in commercial nuclear reactors. However, major cost overruns and schedule slippages have led to a re-examination of how best to achieve this goal. Multiple independent analyses confirm that the MOX approach would be significantly more expensive than originally anticipated and would require approximately $800 million to $1 billion annually for decades. It would be irresponsible to pursue this approach when a more cost-effective alternative exists.

In 2018, after factoring in termination costs for the MFFF project and pursuing the D&D strategy, this proposal generates a net cost savings of $61 million compared to constructing the MFFF. Over the life of the project, comparing current cost estimates for the MFFF and D&D, this proposal will avoid up to an additional $5 billion to $9 billion in construction costs and billions more in operating costs while disposing of the surplus plutonium more quickly.

ELIMINATION: AGENCY FOR HEALTHCARE RESEARCH AND QUALITY
Department of Health and Human Services

The Budget proposes to consolidate the Agency for Healthcare Research and Quality's (AHRQ) activities in the National Institutes of Health (NIH). This consolidation will reduce duplication and leverage the expertise of both AHRQ and NIH.

Funding Summary
(In millions of dollars)

	2017 CR	2018 Request	2018 Change from 2017
Budget Authority..	333	0	-333

Note: The 2018 Request includes $272 million within NIH to consolidate AHRQ's activities within NIH.

Justification

AHRQ, which has not been authorized since 2005, has had a mandate to enhance the quality, appropriateness, and effectiveness of health services through research and promotion of best practices to improve health systems and outcomes. However, other agencies also conduct health services research and promote best practices that improve delivery of care and enhance patient safety. In particular, NIH already conducts $1.5 billion in health services research, but it is conducted by individual institutes across NIH. Consolidating AHRQ into NIH will reduce duplication and improve the effectiveness of existing health services research. The Budget proposes that NIH will conduct a review of health services research across NIH, identify gaps, and propose a more coordinated strategy for ensuring that the highest priority health services research is conducted and then made available to improve the quality of health care services.

ELIMINATION: COMMUNITY SERVICES BLOCK GRANT
Department of Health and Human Services

The Budget eliminates the Community Services Block Grant (CSBG) because it constitutes a small portion of the funding these grantees receive, and funds are not directly tied to performance, which limits incentives for innovation. CSBG also funds some services that are duplicative of services that are funded through other Federal programs, such as emergency food assistance funded through the Department of Agriculture's The Emergency Food Assistance Program (TEFAP) and workforce programs funded through the Departments of Education and Labor.

Funding Summary
(In millions of dollars)

	2017 CR	2018 Request	2018 Change from 2017
Budget Authority..	714	0	-714

Justification

CSBG funds approximately 1,000 nonprofit organizations, local governments, tribal organizations, and migrant and seasonal farm worker organizations commonly referred to as Community Action Agencies (CAAs). CSBG funding is not well targeted, since funding is allocated to States based only on the historical share of funding States received in 1981. Furthermore, funding is distributed by a formula that is not directly tied to performance so it is difficult to ensure funds are spent effectively, which also limits incentives for innovation. CAAs also receive funding from a variety of sources other than CSBG, including from other Federal sources. This program is unauthorized.

REDUCTION: FOOD AND DRUG ADMINISTRATION MEDICAL PRODUCT USER FEES
Department of Health and Human Services

The Budget recalibrates the level of Food and Drug Administration (FDA) medical product user fees to over $2.4 billion in 2018, approximately $1.2 billion over 2017 annualized CR level, replacing the need for new appropriated funding to cover pre-market review costs. To complement the increase in medical product user fees, the Budget also announces several administrative actions designed to achieve regulatory efficiency and speed the development of safe and effective medical products.

Funding Summary
(In millions of dollars)

	2017 CR	2018 Request	2018 Change from 2017
Prescription Drug Program	321	0	-321
Medical Device Program	243	0	-243
Generic Drug Program	121	0	-121
Biosimilar Program	32	0	-32
Animal Drug Program	46	0	-46
Animal Generic Drug Program	6	0	-6
Total Budget Authority	769	0	-769

Note: Amounts in the table reflect the portion of the $1.2 billion increase in user fees that would replace appropriated budget authority.

Justification

The Budget proposes to increase medical product user fees to finance the full cost of FDA pre-market review and replace the need for new appropriated budget authority. Currently, medical product user fees cover an average of 60 percent of FDA premarket review costs, ranging from 30 percent for animal drug review to 70 percent for prescription drugs. Ensuring that FDA has the capacity to carry out its mission is a priority for the Administration. Industries that directly benefit from FDA's medical product premarket approval and administrative actions can and should pay more to support FDA's continued capacity.

The Budget also includes a package of administrative actions that will promote regulatory efficiency and speed the development of safe and effective medical products. These actions include:

1) Encouraging the use of 21st Century Cures Act tools for drug evaluation, review, and approval;

2) Simplifying administrative requirements to reduce drug and device manufacturers' reporting burden;

3) Clarifying treatment of value-based purchasing arrangements; and

4) Improving predictability for payers and enhancing dissemination of evidence by fostering the exchange of scientifically sound information between manufacturers and payers' pre-approval to reduce uncertainty and improve payer ability to more accurately set premiums.

ELIMINATION: HEALTH PROFESSIONS AND NURSING TRAINING PROGRAMS
Department of Health and Human Services

The Budget eliminates health professions and nursing training programs that lack evidence of significantly improving the Nation's health workforce. The Budget continues to fund health workforce activities that provide scholarships and loan repayments in exchange for service in areas of the United States where there is a shortage of health professionals.

Funding Summary
(In millions of dollars)

	2017 CR	2018 Request	2018 Change from 2017
Budget Authority	491	88	-403

Justification

The Budget eliminates funding for 14 health professions and nurse training programs that provide funds to training institutions to improve the quantity, quality, diversity, and/or distribution of the Nation's health workforce. These programs have been in existence for decades and most operate under expired authorizations. There is little evidence that these programs significantly improve the Nation's health workforce. For example, less than half of the physician and physician assistant graduates from the Primary Care Training and Enhance Program practice in medically underserved areas. There are many Federal programs that support the training of health care professionals. A Government Accountability Office report found that four Federal departments, the Departments of Health and Human Services, Veterans Affairs, Defense, and Education, administered 91 programs that supported postsecondary training or education specifically for direct care health professionals.[1] The Budget continues to invest in health care workforce activities that directly place health care providers in areas of the country where they are most needed. For example, the Budget supports the NURSE Corps and proposes new funding for the National Health Service Corps. These programs provide scholarships or repay educational loans for health professionals that agree to work in areas experiencing a shortage of health care providers. The Budget also includes funding to support graduate medical education in high needs areas, including teaching health centers located in underserved areas and children's hospitals.

Citations

[1] Government Accountability Office, Health Care Workforce: *Federal Investments in Training and the Availability of Data for Workforce Projections*, GAO-14-510T, (2014).

ELIMINATION: LOW INCOME HOME ENERGY ASSISTANCE PROGRAM
Department of Health and Human Services

The Budget proposes to eliminate the Low Income Home Energy Assistance Program (LIHEAP) in order to reduce the size and scope of the Federal Government and better target resources within the Department of Health and Human Services' Administration for Children and Families.

Funding Summary
(In millions of dollars)

	2017 CR	2018 Request	2018 Change from 2017
Budget Authority	3,384	0	-3,384

Justification

LIHEAP is a Federal program that has been known to have sizeable fraud and abuse, leading to program integrity concerns. Specifically, a 2010 Government Accountability Office (GAO) study concluded that the program lacked proper oversight, which resulted in significant improper payments. In particular, the report highlighted a number of incidents in which program funds were distributed to deceased or incarcerated individuals. In addition, the report also determined that LIHEAP application processors did little to prevent awards from being provided to individuals with fake addresses and fake energy bills. Since the report, States have taken steps to work towards improving the verification of identify and income.

Perhaps more notably, the Budget recognizes the program is no longer a necessity as States have adopted their own policies to protect constituents against energy concerns. Since LIHEAP was created in 1981, many States have enacted so-called "disconnection policies." In fact, all 50 States and the District of Columbia have imposed regulations that prevent utility companies from disconnecting energy needs from their residents under certain circumstances. In total, 15 of those States enforce temperature restrictions related to freezing and/or extreme heat weather. Other States use date-specific criteria. For example, Minnesota utilizes a "Cold Weather Rule," which requires utility companies to provide electricity and gas during the coldest months, from October 15 until April 15.

Citations

1. Government Accountability Office, Low-Income Home Energy Assistance Program: Greater Fraud Prevention Controls Are Needed, GAO-10-621 (June 2010)

REDUCTION: NATIONAL INSTITUTE FOR OCCUPATIONAL SAFETY AND HEALTH
Department of Health and Human Services

The Budget funds critical research conducted by the National Institute for Occupational Safety and Health (NIOSH) and proposes to eliminate the Education and Research Centers (ERCs) and other activities where NIOSH does not have enforcement action, or where the private sector or other Federal partners could more effectively conduct these activities. The Budget prioritizes core public health activities and reduces programs that have less of a public health impact such as the NIOSH.

Funding Summary
(In millions of dollars)

	2017 CR	2018 Request	2018 Change from 2017
Budget Authority	338	200	-138

Justification

NIOSH was created in 1970 to ensure safe and healthful working conditions for Americans, including mine safety research. The ERCs were created in the 1970s to develop occupational health and safety training programs in academic institutions. Almost 50 years later, the majority of schools of public health include coursework and many academic institutions have developed specializations in these areas. The Budget would stop direct Federal funding to support academic salaries, stipends, and tuition and fee reimbursements for occupational health professionals at universities. Activities conducted by NIOSH could be more effectively conducted by the private sector. For example, NIOSH collects and quantifies human body size and the shape of various occupational groups to develop equipment designs for worker protection. The private sector also conducts similar research in the development of ergonomic equipment.

REDUCTION: NATIONAL INSTITUTES OF HEALTH TOPLINE
Department of Health and Human Services

The Budget proposes to reduce funding for the National Institutes of Health (NIH) to better target funding to support the highest priority biomedical research.

Funding Summary
(In millions of dollars)

	2017 CR	2018 Request	2018 Change from 2017
Budget Authority	31,674	25,883	-5,791

Justification

In 2018, NIH would receive nearly $26 billion to improve public health by advancing our knowledge of disease and cures. NIH would improve agency management by reducing duplication, and reducing both agency and grantee administrative costs.

The Budget proposes NIH structural reforms, including the elimination of the Fogarty International Center which supports international research capacity and training of researchers overseas. International research will be prioritized, as appropriate, by other NIH Institutes as part of their research portfolios. For example, NIH's National Institute of Allergy and Infectious Disease conducts international research that has important implications for U.S. health improvements. However, duplicative and unnecessary global health research will be curtailed.

The Budget also proposes to reduce reimbursement of grantee administrative and facilities costs, referred to as "indirect costs", so that available funding can be better targeted toward supporting the highest priority research on diseases that affect human health. As a result of these changes to the reimbursement structure, significant reductions in 2018 will come from lower indirect cost payments. Increasing efficiencies within the NIH is a priority of the Administration. The Budget includes an indirect cost rate for NIH grants that will be capped at 10 percent of total research. This approach would be applied to all types of grants with a rate higher than 10 percent currently and will achieve significant savings in 2018. It would also bring NIH's reimbursement rate for indirect costs more in line with the reimbursement rate used by private foundations, such as the Gates Foundation, for biomedical research conducted at U.S. universities. In addition, the Budget proposes that NIH will streamline select Federal research requirements for grantees through targeted approaches. In tandem, the Budget supports burden reduction measures that will further reduce grant award recipient costs associated with research.

REDUCTION: OFFICE OF THE NATIONAL COORDINATOR FOR HEALTH INFORMATION TECHNOLOGY
Department of Health and Human Services

The Budget proposes to restructure the Office of the National Coordinator for Health Information Technology (ONC) by reducing its budget by 36 percent and focusing resources on the highest health information technology (IT) priorities.

Funding Summary
(In millions of dollars)

	2017 CR	2018 Request	2018 Change from 2017
Budget Authority	60	38	-22

Justification

ONC is the principal Federal entity charged with coordinating nationwide efforts to implement and use the most advanced health IT and the electronic exchange of health information. When ONC was created, a small minority of physicians and hospitals used health information technology. Now that the vast majority of physicians and hospitals have adopted electronic health records through Federal incentive payments, it is time for a renewed, more focused role for ONC. For example, ONC will work with private sector entities to help create an environment that allows for the successful implementation of health IT. A restructured ONC will maintain a focus on core health IT functions, such as policy development and coordination and standards and certification activities. The Budget would eliminate or significantly reduce lower-priority activities or activities that can be performed by other entities. The Budget also would reduce administrative costs. These changes would improve ONC's ability to be an effective coordinator of nationwide health IT activities and increase the Agency's efficiencies.

REDUCTION: FEDERAL EMERGENCY MANAGEMENT AGENCY STATE AND LOCAL GRANTS
Department of Homeland Security

The Budget proposes to reduce the Federal Emergency Management Agency's (FEMA) grants to State and local governments by $767 million. These savings are generated by certain proposed eliminations, as well as a proposed cost share. A 25 percent non-Federal cost match is proposed for certain grant programs that currently do not require one. Federal resources must be targeted to those activities that provide clear results and that do not supplant State and local responsibilities.

Funding Summary
(In millions of dollars)

	2017 CR	2018 Request	2018 Change from 2017
Cost Share	1,065	798	-267
Reduction	635	414	-221
Elimination	279	0	-279
Total	1,979	1,212	-767

Justification

The Budget proposes eliminating funding for FEMA's Continuing Training Grants, National Domestic Preparedness Consortium (NDPC), Countering Violent Extremism (CVE) / Complex Coordinated Terrorist Attack (CCTA) Grants, and Emergency Food and Shelter Program. These programs are proposed for elimination because they are duplicative of other Federal programs and are primarily State and local responsibilities. Continuing Training Grants and the NDPC are proposed for elimination because other grant funds to State and local entities can be used to pay for training activities for first responders, and because they are duplicative of FEMA's Emergency Management Institute and Center for Domestic Preparedness. The CVE/CCTA grants are proposed for elimination because program costs are eligible under the State Homeland Security Grant Program (SHSGP) and the Urban Area Security Initiative (UASI). The Emergency Food and Shelter Program is proposed for elimination because it is duplicative of Federal housing programs administered by the Department of Housing and Urban Development and because emergency food and shelter is primarily a State and local responsibility.

The Budget further proposes to reduce funding for Emergency Management Performance Grants (EMPG), the Pre-Disaster Mitigation (PDM) Grant Program, the SHSGP, the UASI, Port Security Grants, and Transit Security Assistance. The budget proposes a 25 percent non-Federal cost match for grant programs that currently do not require one (SHSGP and UASI) in order to share accountability for grant dollars with State and local partners and to align with other FEMA grant programs. The Budget also proposes reductions to unauthorized programs (Port Security Grants and Transit Security Assistance). Other reductions to State and local grants are proposed in order to ensure adequate funding for core Department of Homeland Security missions, encourage grant recipients to begin to incorporate the full cost of preparedness activities into their own budgets, and fund those activities that demonstrate the greatest return on security investments.

In each of the past three fiscal years, FEMA's State and local grant programs received more than $2 billion, a generous pipeline of funding that, when combined with the $1.2 billion requested in the Budget, will ensure adequate resources for State and local projects for the foreseeable future. Of the $4 billion in awards made since 2013, recipients of FEMA's two largest grant programs - SHSGP and UASI - are currently carrying more than $1.9 billion in unspent balances, or 47 percent of awarded funds. The Federal Government cannot afford to over-invest in programs that State and local partners are slow to utilize when there are other pressing needs.

ELIMINATION: FLOOD HAZARD MAPPING AND RISK ANALYSIS PROGRAM
Department of Homeland Security

The Budget proposes eliminating the discretionary appropriation for the National Flood Insurance Program's (NFIP's) Flood Hazard Mapping Program (RiskMAP). Instead of discretionary appropriations funded by the taxpayer, FEMA would explore other more effective and fair means of funding flood mapping efforts.

Funding Summary
(In millions of dollars)

	2017 CR	2018 Request	2018 Change from 2017
Budget Authority	190	0	-190

Justification

FEMA maintains quality flood hazard information and develops Flood Insurance Rate Maps (FIRMs, or flood maps) to inform decisions related to flood risk. FEMA has mapped 1.13 million stream miles covering 98 percent of the population in the United States. Flood maps communicate flood risks to communities and residents, inform local floodplain management regulations, help communities set minimum floodplain and building standards, determine who is required to purchase flood insurance, and help FEMA to accurately price flood insurance.

Since flood maps most benefit NFIP policyholders and communities at risk of flooding, mapping costs should be borne by flood insurance policyholders, not general taxpayers. To complement FEMA's efforts, State and local governments can also invest their own resources in updating flood maps to inform land use decisions and reduce risk.

ELIMINATION: TRANSPORTATION SECURITY ADMINISTRATION LAW ENFORCEMENT GRANTS

Department of Homeland Security

The Budget proposes to eliminate funding that incentivizes State and local law enforcement entities to provide law enforcement at airports by partially reimbursing those entities. This incentive is no longer necessary nearly 16 years after the September 11, 2001 attacks, as State and local jurisdictions have had plenty of time to adjust and reprioritize resources.

Funding Summary
(In millions of dollars)

	2017 CR	2018 Request	2018 Change from 2017
Budget Authority	45	0	-45

Justification

The Transportation Security Administration provides assistance to State and local law enforcement jurisdictions to partially reimburse law enforcement activity currently at airports. The program was created to encourage law enforcement presence at airports in the wake of the September 11, 2011 attacks, and to lessen the burden on State and local jurisdictions as they refocused law enforcement efforts. In the 16 years since those attacks, airport security continues to be a high priority not just for the Federal government, but also for the State and local communities whose economies benefit from aviation. This continued state of affairs indicates that no incentive should be necessary for State and local law enforcement entities to prioritize security at their airports.

The amount of financial support offered by this program has waned in recent years, declining below 50 percent of total State and local law enforcement costs in fiscal year 2016 and continuing to decline. As such, State and local jurisdictions are supporting much more of the cost of providing law enforcement presence at airports. Discontinuing this program should not place an undue burden on State and local jurisdictions, since they already pay the majority of law enforcement costs.

ELIMINATION: CHOICE NEIGHBORHOODS
Department of Housing and Urban Development

The Budget proposes to eliminate funding for the Choice Neighborhoods program, recognizing a greater role for State and local governments and the private sector to address community revitalization needs.

Funding Summary
(In millions of dollars)

	2017 CR	2018 Request	2018 Change from 2017
Budget Authority	125	0	-125

Justification

Choice Neighborhoods provides competitive planning and implementation grants to improve neighborhoods with distressed public and/or assisted housing. In addition to providing a direct investment, this unauthorized program leverages additional private and public funds.[1] While leveraging private resources is desirable, early reports suggest that many of the funds leveraged by Choice grantees were existing commitments and appear as if they would have occurred in the absence of a Choice grant.[2] Furthermore, examples of Choice grants catalyzing additional resources beyond housing finance, like infrastructure or safety resources needed for neighborhood improvement, were infrequent.[3]

State and local governments may be better positioned to fund locally-driven strategies for neighborhood revitalization. Moreover, local government's commitment to policy changes and interagency coordination are critical to achieving the educational and public safety goals associated with the program, and to achieve the necessary scale to impact entire neighborhoods.[4]

Citations

[1] U.S. Department of Housing and Urban Development: *Choice Neighborhoods 2015 Grantee Report*, (January 2016).

[2] U.S. Department of Housing and Urban Development: *Developing Choice Neighborhoods: An Early Look at Implementation in Five Sites*, (September 2013).

[3] U.S. Department of Housing and Urban Development: *Choice Neighborhoods: Baseline Conditions and Early Progress*, (September 2015).

[4] U.S. Department of Housing and Urban Development: *Choice Neighborhoods: Baseline Conditions and Early Progress*, (September 2015).

ELIMINATION: COMMUNITY DEVELOPMENT BLOCK GRANT
Department of Housing and Urban Development

The Budget proposes to eliminate funding for the Community Development Block Grant (CDBG) program. The program is not well-targeted to the poorest populations and has not demonstrated a measurable impact on communities.

Funding Summary
(In millions of dollars)

	2017 CR	2018 Request	2018 Change from 2017
Budget Authority	2,994	0	-2,994

Justification

CDBG provides flexible formula funds to 1,250 State and local grantees to support a wide range of community and economic development activities (e.g., housing rehabilitation, blight removal, infrastructure and public improvements, public services). The Federal Government has spent over $150 billion on CDBG since its inception in 1974, but the program has not demonstrated results. The broad purpose and flexible nature of this unauthorized program allows for a wide range of community activities to be supported, but it is this same flexibility that creates challenges to measuring the program's impact and efficacy in improving communities.

The program has largely remained unchanged since it was last reauthorized in 1994. Studies have shown that the allocation formula poorly targets funds to the areas of greatest need, and many aspects of the program have become outdated.[1] Moreover, decreasing appropriations combined with an increasing number of localities qualifying for CDBG allocations has reduced the size of the individual grants over time, making CDBG less impactful.

The Budget recognizes that State and local governments are better positioned to address local community and economic development needs.

Citations

[1] Housing Policy Debate: *CDBG at 40: Its Record and Potential,* Volume 24, Issue 1, (2014).

REDUCTION: GRANTS TO NATIVE AMERICAN TRIBES AND ALASKA NATIVE VILLAGES

Department of Housing and Urban Development

The Budget proposes to reduce overall Department of Housing and Urban Development (HUD) funding targeted to Native American Tribes and Alaskan Native villages. The Budget proposes $600 million for the Native American Housing Block Grant (NAHBG) program and redirects the savings to higher priority areas. The Budget also proposes to eliminate the Indian Community Development Block Grant (ICDBG) because it is duplicative.

Funding Summary
(In millions of dollars)

	2017 CR	2018 Request	2018 Change from 2017
Native American Housing Block Grant	648	600	-48
Indian Community Development Block Grant	60	0	-60
Total	708	600	-108

Justification

NAHBG provides formula grants to Native American Tribes and Alaska Native villages ("Tribes") for affordable housing and related activities. The Budget proposes that funding for this unauthorized program be reduced and redirected to programs in higher priority areas, such as national security and public safety. While the program is fulfilling its mission by increasing the stock of affordable housing in Indian Country, improved data collection is necessary to assess grantee performance on efficiency metrics. For example, we cannot say whether grantees are keeping vacancies to a minimum or turning vacant units over quickly.

ICDBG provides competitive grants to Tribes for a range of projects, including the construction and rehabilitation of affordable housing, community facilities, and infrastructure. The Budget proposes to eliminate ICDBG as it is unauthorized and duplicates, in part, HUD's larger NAHBG program and the Department of Agriculture's Rural Economic Infrastructure Grants, the Department of Transportation's Tribal Transportation Program, and the Environmental Protection Agency's Clean Water and Drinking Water State Revolving Funds.

ELIMINATION: HOME INVESTMENT PARTNERSHIPS PROGRAM
Department of Housing and Urban Development

The Budget proposes to eliminate the HOME Investment Partnerships Program, recognizing a greater role for State and local governments and the private sector in addressing affordable housing needs.

Funding Summary
(In millions of dollars)

	2017 CR	2018 Request	2018 Change from 2017
Budget Authority	948	0	-948

Justification

The HOME Investment Partnerships Program provides flexible formula grants to 600 States and localities to expand the supply of affordable housing for low-income households. Program funding has not been authorized since 1994.

Housing for low-income families is currently funded by multiple funding sources, including Federal, State, and local governments, as well as the private and non-profit sectors. The result is a fragmented system with varying rules and regulations that create overlap and inefficiencies, as well as challenges to measuring collective performance.[1] The Administration devolves affordable housing activities to State and local governments who are better positioned to comprehensively address the array of unique market challenges, local policies, and impediments that lead to housing affordability problems.

Citations

[1] Government Accountability Office: *Affordable Rental Housing: Assistance Is Provided by Federal, State, and Local Programs, but There Is Incomplete Information on Collective Performance*, GAO-15-645, (September 2015).

REDUCTION: RENTAL ASSISTANCE PROGRAMS
Department of Housing and Urban Development

The Budget proposes legislative reforms to reduce costs across the Department of Housing and Urban Development's (HUD) rental assistance programs. The proposed policies include administrative relief and streamlining for grantees, as well as policies that encourage work and self-sufficiency, including increases to tenant rent contributions.

Funding Summary
(In millions of dollars)

	2017 CR	2018 Request	2018 Change from 2017
Budget Authority	37,162	35,228	-1,934

Justification

HUD's rental assistance programs (Housing Choice Vouchers, Public Housing, Project-Based Rental Assistance, and Housing for the Elderly and Persons with Disabilities) provide housing subsidies for about 4.5 million very low-income households. The rental assistance programs generally comprise about 80 percent of HUD's total funding. Due to rent and utility inflation, program costs increase every year just to assist roughly the same number of households.

Given the significant size of the Federal commitment, the Budget proposes a set of policies that would reduce costs and serve as a starting point for a more comprehensive package of rental assistance reforms. The Budget also recognizes the need for greater contributions from State and local governments and the private sector to help address affordable housing needs among low-income households.

ELIMINATION: SELF-HELP AND ASSISTED HOMEOWNERSHIP OPPORTUNITY PROGRAM ACCOUNT

Department of Housing and Urban Development

The Budget proposes to eliminate small grant programs that are duplicative or overlap with other Federal, State, and local efforts. The Budget also recognizes a greater role for State, and local governments and the private sector in addressing community development and affordable housing needs.

Funding Summary
(In millions of dollars)

	2017 CR	2018 Request	2018 Change from 2017
Budget Authority	56	0	-56

Justification

The Budget eliminates the programs in the Self-Help and Assisted Homeownership Opportunity Program (SHOP) account, including SHOP, Capacity Building for Community Development and Affordable Housing program (also known as Section 4), and the rural capacity building program. These programs represent a small fraction of the funds provided by other Federal, State, local, and private entities to support housing and community development activities. The non-profit organizations that receive these grants should have the capacity to substitute funding through more flexible funding from the private sector and philanthropy. For example:

SHOP. SHOP is a competitive grant program that provides funds to non-profit organizations to assist low-income homebuyers willing to contribute "sweat equity" toward the construction of their homes. This unauthorized program expired in 2001, and funding is eliminated and redirected to other higher priority activities.

Capacity Building. Section 4 funding was last authorized in 1996, and the program is effectively an earmark for three organizations. The rural capacity building program is also unauthorized. HUD has adopted a more integrated and efficient approach to technical assistance and strengthening grantees in recent years, and will align these programs' activities with those efforts, as appropriate.

ELIMINATION: ABANDONED MINE LAND GRANTS
Department of the Interior

The Budget proposes to eliminate funding introduced in 2016 for grants to Appalachian States for economic development projects in conjunction with coal abandoned mine land (AML) reclamation. These grants exceed the mission and expertise of the Office of Surface Mining Reclamation and Enforcement (OSMRE).

Funding Summary
(In millions of dollars)

	2017 CR	2018 Request	2018 Change from 2017
Budget Authority	90	0	-90

Justification

The AML grant pilot program was developed by the Congress in response to the prior administration's 2016 Budget mandatory grant proposal to convert $1 billion from the unappropriated balance of the AML Fund to funding for States to expedite the cleanup and redevelopment of eligible lands and waters affected by historic coal mining practices and thus promote economic development. The Congress subsequently appropriated from General Funds $90 million in 2016 discretionary funding for these activities in three Appalachian states (Kentucky, West Virginia, and Pennsylvania). OSMRE's expertise is in coal mine reclamation and not economic development, so it would have to build capacity and leverage expertise from other agencies to implement this approach. These unnecessary grants are not central to OSMRE's mission. Although well intended, these grants overlap with existing funds to reclaim abandoned coal mines and do not have a clearly defined purpose. The Administration plans to help coal country by streamlining permit approvals and eliminating unnecessary regulations, such as lifting the moratorium on coal leasing on public lands, rolling back the Clean Power Plan, and helping to nullify the Stream Protection Rule. The Budget also proposes funding increases for the Appalachian region, including $80 million as part of a new Department of Agriculture Rural Economic Infrastructure Grant account and an additional $66 million in the Department of Labor's Dislocated Worker National Reserve for job training and employment services to help unemployed workers in the region.

REDUCTION: FEDERAL LAND ACQUISITION
Department of the Interior

The Budget proposes to reduce Federal land acquisition funding for the Department of the Interior (DOI) to $54 million. This allows the Agency to focus available funds on the protection and management of existing lands and assets.

Funding Summary
(In millions of dollars)

	2017 CR	2018 Request	2018 Change from 2017
Budget Authority	183	54	-129

Justification

The Budget proposes a reduction of $129 million for Federal land acquisition through DOI, so that the Agency can instead focus limited resources to more effectively manage existing assets and lands. Land acquisitions at DOI are lower priority activities than maintaining adequate funding for ongoing operations and maintenance. DOI already owns roughly 500 million acres of Federal land. At a time when DOI has billions of dollars in deferred maintenance, it needs to focus scarce resources and better manage what it owns before acquiring additional lands.

ELIMINATION: HERITAGE PARTNERSHIP PROGRAM
Department of the Interior

The Budget proposes to eliminate grant funding for the Heritage Partnership Program, a $19 million reduction. This program provides financial and technical assistance to congressionally designated National Heritage Areas, which are managed by non-Federal organizations to promote the conservation of natural, historic, scenic, and cultural resources. The Program is secondary to the primary mission of the National Park Service and would be better sustained with local funding.

Funding Summary
(In millions of dollars)

	2017 CR	2018 Request	2018 Change from 2017
Budget Authority	20	1	-19

Justification

As noted in a Government Accountability Office report, there is no systematic process for designating Heritage Partnership Areas or determining their effectiveness.[1] A Heritage Foundation report raised concerns that these grants are diverting resources from core National Park Service responsibilities, such as protecting resources and providing services in national parks.[2] These grants to State and local entities are not clearly a Federal responsibility; instead, National Heritage Area managers should use the national designation to open doors to more sustainable funding opportunities from local and private beneficiaries.

Citations

[1] Barry T. Hill, Director, Natural Resources and Environment, U.S. General Accounting Office: *National Park Service: A More Systematic Process for Establishing National Heritage Areas and Actions to Improve Their Accountability Are Needed*, testimony before the Committee on Energy and Natural Resources, U.S. Senate, GAO-04-593T, (March 30, 2004).

[2] Heritage Foundation: *National Heritage Areas: Costly Economic Development Schemes that Threaten Property Rights*, Cheryl Chumley and Ronald Utt, (October 23, 2007).

ELIMINATION: NATIONAL WILDLIFE REFUGE FUND
Department of the Interior

The Budget proposes to eliminate discretionary funding for the National Wildlife Refuge Fund. This Fund was intended to compensate communities for lost tax revenue from Federal land acquisitions, but fails to take into account the economic benefits refuges provide to communities.

Funding Summary
(In millions of dollars)

	2017 CR	2018 Request	2018 Change from 2017
Budget Authority	13	0	-13

Justification

Though the National Wildlife Refuge Fund was intended to compensate communities for lost tax revenue from Federal land acquisitions, evidence shows that refuges often generate tax revenue for communities in excess of what was lost by increasing property values and creating tourism opportunities for the American public to connect with nature. In 2013, refuges generated an estimated $2.4 billion for local economies, supported over 35,000 jobs, and generated over $340 million in tax revenues at the local, State, and Federal level.[1] A study by North Carolina State University in 2012 found that property values surrounding refuges are higher than equivalent property values elsewhere.[2]

In addition, approximately $8 million per year in mandatory appropriations is provided to communities from the National Wildlife Refuge Fund.

Citations

[1] U.S. Fish and Wildlife Service: *Banking on Nature: the Economic Benefits to Local Communities of National Wildlife Refuge Visitation*. (October 2013).

[2] North Carolina State University Center for Environmental and Resource Economic Policy: *Amenity Values of Proximity to National Wildlife Refuges,* (April 2012).

REDUCTION: FEDERAL PRISON SYSTEM, CONSTRUCTION
Department of Justice

The Budget proposes to cancel or redirect $888 million of prison construction funding in order to fund other law enforcement priorities, such as immigration and violent crime. This proposal leverages existing prison capacity resulting from a decline in the inmate population of approximately 30,000 people since 2013.

Funding Summary
(In millions of dollars)

	2017 CR	2018 Request	2018 Change from 2017
Budget Authority	444	-444	-888

Justification

The Congress appropriated $444 million in 2016 for the construction of a new prison. The Budget proposes no new funding for prison construction and proposes to cancel the $444 million in unobligated balances appropriated for construction of the facility.

Rather than investing in new construction, the Budget includes funding to expand prison capacity in more efficient and cost-effective ways. The Budget includes $80 million in the BOP Salaries and Expenses account for activation of AUSP Thomson, which currently houses just 93 inmates at its work camp. At full activation, Thomson has capacity to house between 1,600 and 2,500 inmates.

Finally, the Attorney General recently released guidance reversing a decision to phase out the use of privately-operated contract facilities. In light of that decision and the present size of the inmate population, the Administration has additional, flexible options for confinement that may be used before expending resources for new construction.

ELIMINATION: STATE CRIMINAL ALIEN ASSISTANCE PROGRAM
Department of Justice

The Budget proposes to eliminate the State Criminal Alien Assistance Program (SCAAP) from the Office of Justice Programs within the Department of Justice. SCAAP, which reimburses State, local, and tribal governments for prior year costs associated with incarcerating certain illegal criminal aliens, is unauthorized and poorly targeted. The Administration proposes to instead invest in border enforcement and border security initiatives that will more effectively address the public safety threats posed by criminal aliens.

Funding Summary
(In millions of dollars)

	2017 CR	2018 Request	2018 Change from 2017
Budget Authority	210	0	-210

Justification

This program represents a general revenue transfer to States that neither focuses resources on immigration enforcement nor fully reimburses their detention costs. In 2016, the reimbursement rate was about 17 cents on the dollar, with just four States – California, Florida, New York, and Texas – receiving over two-thirds of available funds. Further, the program has no performance metrics or programmatic requirements associated with the funds to improve public safety. Moreover, the program does not require recipients to use SCAAP awards solely for the purpose of addressing the cost of detaining illegal aliens in State, local and tribal detention facilities.

REDUCTION: BUREAU OF INTERNATIONAL LABOR AFFAIRS
Department of Labor

The Budget proposes to eliminate the Department of Labor's international labor grants and reduce International Labor Affairs Bureau (ILAB) staff, instead focusing ILAB on ensuring that U.S. trade agreements are fair for American workers.

Funding Summary
(In millions of dollars)

	2017 CR	2018 Request	2018 Change from 2017
Budget Authority	86	19	-67

Justification

Despite its role in ensuring that U.S. trade agreements are fair for American workers, ILAB spends almost 70 percent of its budget on grants to combat child labor and promote worker rights overseas. Many of these grants are awarded noncompetitively and are of questionable long-term effectiveness. ILAB has funded some impact evaluations of its child labor projects, but the findings have been mixed. The completed child labor impact evaluations show that education projects had limited effects on withdrawing and preventing children from participating in child labor.[1] The Budget proposes to eliminate these grants and focus ILAB on ensuring that American workers are competing on a level playing field with other countries.

Citations

[1] Government Accountability Office: *International Labor Grants: DOL's Use of Financial and Performance Monitoring Tools Needs to be Strengthened,* GAO-14-832 (September 2014).

ELIMINATION: MIGRANT AND SEASONAL FARMWORKER TRAINING
Department of Labor

The Budget eliminates the Migrant and Seasonal Farmworker Training program (also known as the National Farmworker Jobs Program). The program is duplicative in that it creates a parallel training system for migrant and seasonal farmworkers, despite the fact that these individuals are eligible to receive services through the core Workforce Innovation and Opportunity Act (WIOA) formula programs.

Funding Summary
(In millions of dollars)

	2017 CR	2018 Request	2018 Change from 2017
Budget Authority	82	0	-82

Justification

The Migrant and Seasonal Farmworker Training program provides grants to 52 organizations to provide training, employment, and other services to migrant farmworkers, with the goal of increasing their employment and earnings. The program also awards housing assistance grants to 11 organizations. While the program reports favorable performance results in terms of the share of participants entering employment, the program has not been rigorously evaluated so it is unclear whether these outcomes would have happened in the absence of the program. Those participants who currently receive training and employment services are eligible for similar services through the core WIOA Titles I and III formula programs.

In addition, while grants are competitively awarded, there is inadequate competition and very little grantee turnover. For example, all 52 grantees receiving employment and training grants in 2016 had also been awarded grants in the previous competition, even though their performance was mixed.

REDUCTION: OFFICE OF DISABILITY EMPLOYMENT POLICY
Department of Labor

The Budget proposes $27 million, returning the Office of Disability Employment Policy (ODEP) closer to its core mission of policy development, technical assistance, and dissemination of effective practices to increase the employment of people with disabilities. For 2018, the Budget proposes that ODEP will also begin a demonstration project to test effective interventions to promote greater labor force participation of people with disabilities.

Funding Summary
(In millions of dollars)

	2017 CR	2018 Request	2018 Change from 2017
Budget Authority..	38	27	-11

Justification

The Congress created ODEP in 2001 to bring a heightened focus on disability employment in the Federal Government through policy analysis, technical assistance and development of best practices.

ODEP was tasked with implementing a sustained, coordinated, and aggressive employment strategy to eliminate job barriers for people with disabilities. However, ODEP has since expanded its responsibilities beyond its original mission to include numerous grant programs on a wide range of activities. This includes support services that were duplicative of other offices, such as ODEP's grants for technical assistance for accessible technology and career development in post-secondary education. For 2018, the Budget proposes that ODEP will eliminate duplicative grant making activities and will refocus its efforts on testing, developing, and implementing disability employment policy to increase the recruitment, retention and advancement of people with disabilities.

The Budget also replaces one of ODEP's major initiatives, the Disability Employment Initiative (DEI), that since 2010 has provided grants to State workforce agencies to improve American Job Center capacity to serve individuals with disabilities. The Federal Government already provides substantial funding to States for their workforce system via the WIOA and Employment Service grants and States are required by law to provide reasonable accommodation to individuals with disabilities to ensure that they can participate. In addition, preliminary results suggest that DEI has shown weak impacts: an interim report showed no statistically significant difference between the treatment and control group in terms of wages or employment placement rates.[1]

The Budget redeploys DEI funding for a new demonstration project modeled after Washington State's workers compensation successful Centers of Occupational Health and Education (COHE) program to improve labor force participation and attachment of individuals with temporary injuries and disabilities. The demonstration, which will be run in partnership with the Social Security Administration, will test the effects of implementing key features of the COHE model in other States or municipalities and/or for a broader population beyond workers' compensation. Some of the key features include care and service coordination, population screening and monitoring, increased access and targeted vocational rehabilitation and work supports, workplace accommodations, and technical assistance to healthcare providers and employers. Other optional interventions that could be tested by grantees include additional income support in absence of other temporary disability supports, partial wage support to allow for part-time return-to-work, increased access to specific medical or holistic care, and employer incentives.

Past efforts provided enhanced incentives to pursue work for people with disabilities who spent years out of the labor force. In contrast to previous efforts, this early intervention return-to-work initiative is aimed at helping the individual worker maintain attachment to the labor force and self-sufficiency.

Citations

[1] Social Dynamics, LLC, and Mathematica Policy Research: *DEI Interim Synthesis Report For Year 4,* (August 2016).

ELIMINATION: OSHA TRAINING GRANTS
Department of Labor

The Budget proposes to eliminate the Occupational Safety and Health Administration's (OSHA) Susan Harwood training grants, which are unnecessary and unproven.

Funding Summary
(In millions of dollars)

	2017 CR	2018 Request	2018 Change from 2017
Budget Authority	11	0	-11

Justification

OSHA's Harwood Training Grant program was established in 1978 to provide one- to five-year competitive grants to non-profit organizations to develop and conduct occupational safety and health training programs. OSHA has no evidence that the program is effective, and measures the program's performance in terms of the number of individuals trained. In addition, it is not clear that the training funded by these grants would not happen absent the Federal subsidy. The Budget provides resources for OSHA's compliance assistance activities, including free on-site safety and health consultations for small businesses; cooperative programs to help employers identify and address hazards; and assistance to help employers and workers improve the safety of their workplaces.

ELIMINATION: SENIOR COMMUNITY SERVICE EMPLOYMENT PROGRAM
Department of Labor

The Budget proposes to eliminate the Senior Community Service Employment Program (SCSEP). SCSEP is ineffective in its goal of transitioning seniors into unsubsidized employment.

Funding Summary
(In millions of dollars)

	2017 CR	2018 Request	2018 Change from 2017
Budget Authority	434	0	-434

Justification

SCSEP distributes grants to States and public and private non-profit organizations to provide part-time work experience in community service activities to unemployed low-income persons ages 55 and over.

While the program provides some income support to about 68,000 individuals each year, it fails to meet its other major statutory goals of fostering economic self-sufficiency and moving low-income seniors into unsubsidized employment. In program year 2015 (the most recent year for which data are available), the program placed less than half of participants in unsubsidized jobs and that excludes as many as one-third of individuals who fail to complete the program. With costs of almost $6,500 per participant, it is not a cost-effective mechanism to facilitate community service among older adults. The goal of supporting the self-sufficiency and employment of older workers can continue to be addressed through the Workforce Innovation and Opportunity Act (WIOA) programs.

REDUCTION: WIOA TITLES I AND III FORMULA PROGRAMS (ADULT, YOUTH, DISLOCATED WORKERS, EMPLOYMENT SERVICE)
Department of Labor

The Budget proposes to decrease funding for the Workforce Innovation and Opportunity Act (WIOA) job training and employment service formula programs by 39 percent. In a resource-constrained environment, the Budget would shift responsibility for funding these services to localities, States, and employers.

Funding Summary
(In millions of dollars)

	2017 CR	2018 Request	2018 Change from 2017
Budget Authority	3,474	2,133	-1,341

Justification

Evaluations of Federal workforce programs show a mixed record of effectiveness. Some have found employment and educational gains, while others have shown negligible, or even negative, effects of participating in training programs. In particular, most impact evaluations of Federal workforce programs have not been able to demonstrate long-term earnings gains associated with program participation.

For example, a 1997 study of the Job Training Partnership Act (a predecessor to WIOA) found modest earnings gains for both adult women and men who participated in the program, but found no earnings gains for either female or male youth participants.[1] Most recently, Mathematica's May 2016 interim impact report on the WIA Adult and Dislocated Worker programs did not find positive earnings or employment effects for those participating in training, though it noted that it was premature to draw final conclusions based on these interim findings.[2] The study also notes that participating in training does not increase individuals' ability to obtain employment in a related occupation. In sum, these programs remain unproven.

The Budget would decrease funding for WIOA Title I and III formula programs by $1.3 billion, shifting more responsibility for funding these programs and training American workers to States, localities, and employers and giving them more freedom to design their programs. The Budget also provides States and localities with new flexibility and discretion to serve workers based on the specific training needs of their workforce.

Citations

[1] Bloom et al. *The Benefits and Costs of JTPA Title II-A Programs: Key Findings from the National Job Training Partnership Act Study*, (1997).

[2] McConnell et al. *Providing Public Workforce Services to Job Seekers: 15 Month Impact Findings on the WIA Adult and Dislocated Worker Programs*, (2016).

ELIMINATION: DEVELOPMENT ASSISTANCE
Department of State and U.S. Agency for International Development

The Budget refocuses and reduces economic and development assistance across countries and sectors in order to prioritize countries of greatest strategic importance and ensure the effectiveness of U.S. taxpayer investments. The Budget proposes to eliminate the Development Assistance account, and selected countries and programs previously covered by the account will be supported through the new Economic Support and Development Fund.

Funding Summary
(In millions of dollars)

	2017 CR	2018 Request	2018 Change from 2017
Budget Authority	2,509	0	-2,509

Note: This table does not include direct climate-change activities funded in the FY 2017 level out of the Development Assistance account. This funding is addressed separately as part of the Global Climate Change Initiative elimination.

Justification

Consistent with the Administration's goals of streamlining foreign assistance and freeing up funding for rebuilding the Nation's military and for pursuing critical priorities here at home, the Budget eliminates the Development Assistance (DA) account and reduces the number of countries receiving direct bilateral economic and development assistance by more than 40 (or by nearly 45) percent compared to 2016, in order to focus on those that are most critical to U.S. national security. Selected countries and programs previously covered by the DA account will be supported through the Economic Support and Development Fund (ESDF), allowing the Department of State (State) and U.S. Agency for International Development (USAID) to better assess, prioritize, and target development-related activities in the context of broader U.S. strategic objectives and partnerships around the world. Having one streamlined account for economic and development assistance will also increase State and USAID's flexibility to trade-off needs on an even footing within one account, rather than having budget and strategic priorities skewed by artificial distinctions. As a result, the Budget refocuses economic and development assistance on countries and sectors that will have the most immediate and direct benefits toward strengthening U.S. national and homeland security, defeating ISIS and other transnational terrorist groups, fostering economic opportunities and opening markets for U.S. businesses, and supporting key strategic partners and allies. Within these countries and sectors, the Budget proposes that State and USAID increase the effectiveness of assistance while reducing expenditures by leveraging strategic partnerships across the Federal Government, international organizations, foreign governments, the private sector, and non-governmental and faith-based organizations. The Budget also proposes that State and USAID strengthen agency processes to monitor and ensure strong programmatic impacts and will apply data-driven analyses to prioritize programs with demonstrated transformative potential.

ELIMINATION: EARMARKED APPROPRIATIONS FOR NON-PROFIT ORGANIZATIONS
Department of State and U.S. Agency for International Development

The Budget proposes to eliminate earmarked appropriations for the East-West Center and The Asia Foundation given these organizations serve niche missions that duplicate other Federal programs. Elimination of earmarked Federal funding will not terminate these organizations, due to their non-profit status, and they remain eligible and are encouraged to compete for Federal grant funding and may receive private sector contributions.

Funding Summary
(In millions of dollars)

	2017 CR	2018 Request	2018 Change from 2017
The Asia Foundation	17	0	-17
East-West Center	17	0	-17

Justification

The East-West Center (EWC) is a quasi-governmental organization established by the Congress in 1960 and The Asia Foundation (TAF) is a private, non-governmental organization founded in 1954. Even though these organizations remain authorized, it is highly unusual for private organizations to receive a direct appropriation with no direct leadership from the Executive Branch to provide oversight. The Administration is seeking to end dedicated funding for organizations that may effectively serve niche missions, but which are not critical to the conduct of U.S. foreign policy and which duplicate the efforts of other Federal programs or the non-profit and private sectors. By making this change, EWC and TAF will be incentivized to compete for Federal funding which will improve efficiency while minimizing the potential for duplication.

REDUCTION: EDUCATIONAL AND CULTURAL EXCHANGES
Department of State and U.S. Agency for International Development

The Budget reduces Federal funding by half for the Department of State's Educational and Cultural Exchange Programs, including the Bureau of Educational and Cultural Affairs (ECA). The need for federally funded educational and cultural exchanges has decreased significantly given the number of exchange students both coming to the United States and studying abroad without Federal support.

Funding Summary
(In millions of dollars)

	2017 CR	2018 Request	2018 Change from 2017
Budget Authority	590	285	-305

Justification

When originally authorized (Mutual Educational and Cultural Exchange Act of 1961), educational and cultural exchanges were an important means of exposing foreign citizens to U.S. culture and U.S. citizens to foreign culture. However, in today's more mobile and interconnected world, students and other international visitors are increasingly relying on other sources of funding and support. For instance, based on Open Doors 2016 data,[1] it is estimated that over one million international students studied at U.S. colleges and universities during the 2015-2016 academic year. Of the total number of international students enrolled during the 2015-2016 academic year, the U.S. Government funded slightly more than 4,000, or 0.4 percent, of international students. The primary sources of funding for international students were personal/family (66 percent) and U.S. colleges and universities (17 percent). In addition, the Open Doors data showed that the total number of U.S. students studying abroad in 2014-2015 was over 300,000. U.S. Government-funded exchange programs support only a small fraction of overall study abroad programs, some of which seek to increase mutual understanding between the United States and other countries. It is clear that the need for U.S. Federal assistance for exchange programs has dropped over time as alternative sources of funding have become more available and the world has become more interconnected due to rapid improvements in transportation and information technology. ECE program resources will be more narrowly targeted towards specific foreign policy priorities while avoiding duplication.

Citations

[1] Institute for International Education: *Research and Insights, Open Doors 2016 Fast Facts*, (2016).

REDUCTION: GLOBAL HEALTH PROGRAMS
Department of State and U.S. Agency for International Development

The Budget reduces foreign assistance to refocus on the highest priorities and strategic objectives, and to bring the U.S. share of collective efforts into better balance with the global community. The 2018 funding level will enable the United States to meet its commitments to the Global Fund to Fight AIDS, TB, & Malaria and Gavi, the Vaccine Alliance as well as continue HIV/AIDS antiretroviral treatment for all current patients under the President's Emergency Plan for AIDS Relief (PEPFAR).

Funding Summary
(In millions of dollars)

	2017 CR	2018 Request	2018 Change from 2017
Budget Authority	8,487	6,481	-2,006

Justification

The United States has been the largest donor by far to global HIV/AIDS efforts, providing over half of global donor funding in recent years to combat this epidemic. The Budget reduces funding for several global health programs, including HIV/AIDS, with the expectation that other donors can and should increase their commitments to these causes. Within the proposed budget for PEPFAR, the State Department would prioritize 12 countries in which the United States will continue to work towards epidemic control, while maintaining all current PEPFAR-supported patient levels on treatment across the program. This proposal would allow PEPFAR to continue to achieve impact within a lower budget by reprioritizing resources and leveraging funding from other donors and host country governments.

The Budget proposes $1.13 billion for the Global Fund to Fight AIDS, TB, & Malaria, a reduction of $222 million below the 2017 CR level. This reduction achieves savings while still keeping the United States on track to meet its commitment to match $1 for every $2 provided by other donors for the Global Fund's most recent 5th Replenishment period. To date, other donors have not stepped forward with sufficient matching contributions to maximize the U.S. pledge.

The Budget also realizes one-time savings by proposing to make $323 million in remaining Ebola emergency funds available to support malaria programs ($250 million) and global health security programs ($73 million) to ensure that these priority programs are robustly funded.

The Budget achieves further savings by eliminating funding in the Global Health Programs account for international family planning programs, a reduction of $523 million below the 2017 CR level. The Budget reduces funding for polio programs at USAID. The Government's efforts to eradicate polio continue to be funded within the Centers for Disease Control & Prevention at $165 million. The Budget proposes additional reductions below the 2017 CR level for tuberculosis, nutrition, vulnerable children, and neglected tropical diseases. While the United States will continue significant funding for global health programs, even while refocusing foreign assistance, other stakeholders must do more to contribute their fair share to global health initiatives.

REDUCTION: INTERNATIONAL ORGANIZATION CONTRIBUTIONS
Department of State and U.S. Agency for International Development

The Budget proposes to end or reduce funding for international programs and organizations whose missions do not substantially advance U.S. foreign policy interests or for which the funding burden is not fairly shared amongst members. Funding for these organizations is currently provided in two accounts: dues and other assessed support is through Contributions to International Organizations (CIO), and additional voluntary contributions are provided through International Organizations and Programs (IOP). No funding for the IOP account is requested in the Budget.

Funding Summary
(In millions of dollars)

	2017 CR	2018 Request	2018 Change from 2017
Base Budget Authority	1,680	900	-780
Overseas Contingency Operations	102	96	-6
Total	1,782	996	-786

Justification

The Budget calls for significant reductions in U.S. contributions to international organizations. In order to implement these reductions, the Budget proposes that the Department of State examine options to: (a) reduce the levels of international organizations' budgets, (b) reduce U.S. assessment rates, and/or (c) not pay U.S. assessments in full. Reducing international organizations' budgets and U.S. assessment rates requires agreement by other member States in inter-governmental bodies such as the UN General Assembly. The Budget proposes that the Department examine possible methods for achieving these two objectives. To pursue the third option, the Department would undergo a systematic review to identify organizations where reductions can be achieved while maintaining U.S. national interests. This proposed interagency process would give priority to organizations that most directly support U.S. national security interests and American prosperity. NATO, for instance, would continue to be fully funded. In contrast, funding for organizations that work against U.S. foreign policy interests could be terminated. To the extent the United States decides to pursue continued funding for any of the organizations previously supported via IOP, the Budget assumes that it would do so through the Economic Support and Development Fund and other foreign assistance accounts in 2018.

REDUCTION: OVERSEAS CONTINGENCY OPERATIONS
Department of State and U.S. Agency for International Development

The Budget marks the first step in a multi-year phase-out of Overseas Contingency Operations (OCO) funding for the Department of State and U.S. Agency for International Development (State/USAID) that is not for temporary and extraordinary contingency needs, so as to end the use of OCO as a means to effectively evade budget caps during the annual appropriations process.

Funding Summary
(In millions of dollars)

	2017 CR	2018 Request	2018 Change from 2017
Overseas Contingency Operations	19,195	12,017	-7,178

Note: The 2017 CR total includes $4,300 million enacted in the Further Continuing and Security Assistance Appropriations Act (Public Law 114-254) for counter-ISIS activities.

Justification

State/USAID was first appropriated OCO funding in 2012 to fund temporary and extraordinary needs related to the wars in Iraq and Afghanistan. While needs for such contingency funding have legitimately grown (*e.g.* the conflict in Syria), the use of OCO to fund State/USAID activities has been greatly expanded beyond its original intent, to include critical activities that are neither temporary nor extraordinary, but are instead ongoing and anticipated. Each year during the appropriations process, shifting enduring State/USAID funding from base to OCO results in a cap adjustment that serves as a relief valve to free up funding for other non-defense discretionary (NDD) priorities and relieve the cap pressures faced by all NDD agencies and programs. For instance, the prior administration requested only $7 billion in State/USAID OCO for 2016. However, as a result of the Bipartisan Budget Act (BBA) of 2015, the OCO level ballooned to $14.9 billion annually for 2016 and 2017, a back-door means of circumventing the cap on NDD spending in order to fund other NDD priorities.

While the BBA technically capped State/USAID OCO funding at $14.9 billion, there is no enforcement mechanism. Consequently, the Congress effectively evaded the cap in December 2016 by providing $4.3 billion in supplemental OCO funding for State/USAID in the Further Continuing and Security Assistance Appropriations Act (SAAA) without any offset. This resulted in a 2017 CR level of $19.2 billion in State/USAID OCO funding, or 35 percent of State/USAID's total budget. An additional $1.6 billion was provided in the 2017 Consolidated Appropriations Act, increasing total 2017 OCO funding to $20.8 billion, $5.9 billion above the 2017 BBA OCO cap.

Whereas OCO was originally intended for use in six State/USAID accounts and three countries where the United States was engaged in conflict, it has expanded to 21 accounts and over 50 countries for a wide range of ongoing activities previously funded within the NDD base budget cap. The 2018 Budget reflects the first step in reining in the expansion of OCO funding, with a reduction of over $7 billion from the 2017 CR level, and a scaling back to 14 accounts and approximately 25 countries.

ELIMINATION: P.L. 480 TITLE II FOOD AID
Department of State and U.S. Agency for International Development

The Budget proposes to eliminate the P.L. 480 Title II food aid program (Title II) in order to focus on the highest priority, most efficient and effective foreign assistance and eliminate inefficient, slow, and high-cost programs. The foreign assistance request retains sufficient funding for emergency food assistance in the International Disaster Assistance (IDA) account, which already provides food aid through the most effective means for each crisis and provides U.S. food commodities where they are the most appropriate emergency response.

Funding Summary
(In millions of dollars)

	2017 CR	2018 Request	2018 Change from 2017
Budget Authority	1,713	0	-1,713

Justification

The Title II program provides emergency and development food aid, mainly through the purchase and shipment of U.S. commodities. The Budget focuses humanitarian and development assistance on the highest priorities and eliminates duplicative programs. Providing emergency food aid through IDA has been shown to allow more appropriate and on average more cost effective assistance than Title II food aid. Unlike Title II, IDA is able to adjust to conflict and other situations such as Syria where affected people may be displaced multiple times. Procuring food near crises can save up to two months or more on delivery time and can significantly reduce the costs of food aid. In addition, such purchases and other tools such as cash vouchers, where appropriate, also help support local economies shaken by humanitarian crises, which can lower overall needs. Given limited resources, it is important to focus funding on the most efficient assistance mechanisms. In this case, IDA allows the choice of the right tool at the right time and maximizes the reach of U.S. assistance.

Disproportionate share of global food aid. The United States is the largest provider of emergency food aid, typically accounting for a third or more of all contributions. As the United States refocuses assistance to the highest priority areas, the Budget calls upon other donors to do their fair share.

Slower and more costly. Title II takes an average of four to six months to deliver food aid, which means that food may need to be moved before it is certain that it is needed (such as anticipating whether and how severe a drought may be) or shipments may arrive too late. Using IDA can significantly shorten the delivery time. In recent disasters, IDA has allowed food to arrive within days, not months. While in some cases Title II can be prepositioned to save some time, these additional storage, handling, and delivery costs mean that U.S. taxpayers are paying even more compared to the costs of IDA.

Less efficient than other foreign assistance. Title II requires that at least 20 percent of an annual appropriation (with a minimum of $350 million per year) must be used for development food aid programs. At least 15 percent of the U.S. commodities for these programs must be sold abroad, typically at an average loss of 25 percent or more of the cost. The proceeds of these sales, referred to as monetization, are used to fund development programs, and the loss on these sales is paid for by U.S. taxpayers. Eliminating these programs aligns with the approach taken towards other foreign assistance programs, ensuring that funding can be focused on the highest priorities, on efficiency, and on effectiveness. The U.S. Agency for International Development will continue to fund longer-term food security and nutrition programs through the Economic Support and Development Fund and the Global Health Program.

REDUCTION: PEACEKEEPING
Department of State and U.S. Agency for International Development

The Budget assumes the United States will contribute at or below the statutory cap of 25 percent for United Nations (UN) peacekeeping missions in the Contributions to International Peacekeeping Activities (CIPA) account. The Budget proposes to eliminate funding for duplicative capacity building programs in the Peacekeeping Operations (PKO) account.

Funding Summary
(In millions of dollars)

	2017 CR	2018 Request	2018 Change from 2017
Base Budget Authority	796	391	-405
Overseas Contingency Operations	2,313	1,106	-1,207
Total Budget Authority	3,109	1,497	-1,612

[1] *The amounts in the table combine reductions to the Contributions to International Peacekeeping (CIPA) account and reductions to the Peacekeeping Operations (PKO) account.*

Justification

With over 100,000 personnel and an annual budget close to $8 billion, UN peacekeeping is a powerful tool to address challenges to international peace and security. Unfortunately, at an assessed rate of 28.4 percent, the United States is paying more than its fair share of the cost, particularly when the other four permanent UN Security Council members with veto power are assessed between four and ten percent. Furthermore, reform is needed to create not only more efficient and accountable peacekeeping operations but also ensure that each mission's mandate reflects realities on the ground and is supported by the necessary political will and structures to achieve its objectives.

The Budget request of $1.2 billion for U.S. contributions to UN peacekeeping activities sets the expectation that the UN will rein in costs by reevaluating the design and implementation of peacekeeping missions and sharing the funding burden more fairly among members. This request assumes that the United States would contribute at or below the statutory cap of 25 percent for UN peacekeeping missions. To ensure that budget cuts would be implemented in a responsible manner while maintaining the most crucial and impactful aspects of UN peacekeeping, the Administration is calling on UN Security Council members to join in conducting strategic reviews of each UN peacekeeping mission.

The Budget proposes to eliminate programs in the PKO account, specifically the Africa Peacekeeping Rapid Response Partnership (APRRP) and the PKO portion of the Security Governance Initiative (SGI). APRRP is a duplicative capacity building program intended to enable African countries to rapidly deploy to UN or regional peacekeeping missions. The Budget assumes that existing global capacity building efforts in the PKO account will target resources to support global efforts to increase the number of trained and equipped peacekeepers ready for deployment. Similarly, the Administration views PKO funding for SGI as unnecessary and duplicative of ongoing bilateral assistance programs. The Budget request of $301 million for PKO would continue to support multilateral peacekeeping and regional stability operations that are not funded by the UN, help build operational readiness and sustainment capabilities for partner countries deploying to peace operations, and build the military capacity of regional partners to counter terrorism.

ELIMINATION: GREEN CLIMATE FUND AND GLOBAL CLIMATE CHANGE INITIATIVE
Departments of State/USAID and Treasury

The Budget fulfills the President's pledge to cease payments to the United Nations' climate change programs by proposing to eliminate U.S. funding in 2018 related to the Green Climate Fund and its two precursor Climate Investment Funds, which include the Clean Technology Fund and the Strategic Climate Fund. To better focus on priority strategic objectives and help ensure the appropriate U.S. share of international spending, the Budget also proposes to eliminate the Global Climate Change Initiative (GCCI) and provides no funding for State Department and U.S. Agency for International Development (USAID) bilateral activities with partner countries to directly address climate change.

Funding Summary
(In millions of dollars)

	2017 CR	2018 Request	2018 Change from 2017
Green Climate Fund (State)	998	0	-998
Clean Technology Fund (Treasury)	170	0	-170
Strategic Climate Fund (Treasury)	60	0	-60
Bilateral GCCI (State and USAID)	362	0	-362
Total Base Budget Authority	1,590	0	-1,590

Justification

The President promised during his campaign, and pledged in his "Contract with the American Voter," to cease payments to the United Nations' climate change programs. By proposing to eliminate funding in 2018 related to the Green Climate Fund (GCF) and its two precursor Climate Investment Funds (CIFs), the Budget fulfills that pledge. The CIFs were designed as an interim, precursor funding mechanism to the GCF, and they comprise the Clean Technology Fund and the Strategic Climate Fund. The United States completed its $2 billion commitment to the CIFs in 2016, and the 2018 Budget makes clear that the Administration does not intend to provide any further contributions to them. The Budget also proposes to eliminate the GCCI and associated State Department and USAID bilateral assistance intended primarily to help other countries mitigate the impacts of climate change. America must put the energy needs of American families and businesses first and continue implementing a plan that ensures energy security and economic vitality for decades to come, including by promoting development of the Nation's vast energy resources.

REDUCTION: CAPITAL INVESTMENT GRANTS (NEW STARTS)
Department of Transportation

The Budget proposes to limit funding for the Federal Transit Administration's Capital Investment Program (New Starts) to projects with existing full funding grant agreements only. Future investments in new transit projects would be funded by the localities that use and benefit from these localized projects. Several major metropolitan regions have recently passed multi-billion dollar revenue measures to fund transit projects, and the Administration believes that is the most appropriate way to fund transit expansion and maintenance efforts.

Funding Summary
(In millions of dollars)

	2017 CR	2018 Request	2018 Change from 2017
Budget Authority	2,160	1,232	-928

Justification

The Budget proposes reduced funding for this program, which provides Federal funding for local transit projects that should be funded by States and localities that benefit from their use. Localities are better equipped to scale and design infrastructure investments needed for their communities. Several major metropolitan areas, including Denver, Los Angeles, and Seattle, have already begun to move in this direction by asking residents to approve multi-billion dollar bond measures to speed the delivery of highway and transit investments. These regions realize waiting for Federal grant funding is not the most efficient way to meet their local transportation needs.

Federal resources should be focused on making targeted investments that can leverage private sector investment and incentivize the creation of revenue streams where possible.

REDUCTION: ESSENTIAL AIR SERVICE
Department of Transportation

The Budget proposes to reform the Essential Air Service (EAS) by eliminating discretionary funding and focusing on the remote airports that are most in need of subsidized commercial air service. The proposal will include a mix of reforms, including limits on per-passenger subsidies and higher average daily enplanements.

Funding Summary
(In millions of dollars)

	2017 CR	2018 Request	2018 Change from 2017
Budget Authority	175	0	-175

Justification

The EAS program was originally established as a temporary program nearly 40 years ago to provide subsidized commercial air service to rural airports. Many EAS flights are not full and have high subsidy costs per passenger. Attempts at incrementally reforming the program have not resulted in much change in the cost of EAS. For example, the Department of Transportation has routinely provided waivers to communities that do not meet some of the eligible criteria and attempts at local cost share have not been successful. Further, several EAS eligible communities are relatively close to major airports. Communities that have EAS could be served by other existing modes of transportation, and the Government Accountability Office has also routinely identified reforms in the EAS program in its annual duplication reports.

The Administration is proposing a wholesale redesign of the program, to eliminate the discretionary component of the program and focus the remaining resources on those remote communities in most need of support.

REDUCTION: GRANTS TO AMTRAK
Department of Transportation

The Budget proposes to terminate Federal support for Long Distance services, which consistently suffer from poor on-time performance, serve a small percentage of the population, and generate the vast majority of Amtrak's operating losses.

Funding Summary
(In millions of dollars)

	2017 CR	2018 Request	2018 Change from 2017
Budget Authority	1,404	774	-630

Justification

Amtrak's long distance trains do not serve a vital transportation purpose, and are a vestige of when train service was the only viable transcontinental transportation option. Today communities are served by an expansive aviation, interstate highway, and intercity bus network. The remaining Federal funds for Amtrak are dedicated to Amtrak's Northeast Corridor (NEC) and State-Supported services, which do provide real transportation alternatives for regions.

Long Distance services suffer from poor on-time performance (55 percent in 2016) and account for only 15 percent of Amtrak ridership but 38 percent of train system operating costs. Long distance trains have consistently had a net operating loss (roughly half a billion dollars annually for the past decade) since Amtrak was created in 1971.

Terminating Federal funding for Long Distance services will allow Amtrak to focus its resources – and those appropriated by Congress – on better managing its successful corridor services that provide transportation options within more densely populated regions. For example, Amtrak's Northeast Corridor train services carry the vast majority of the combined air/rail market between Washington and New York. Yet this corridor faces many challenges, and the 2018 Budget proposal would allow Amtrak to right-size itself and more adequately focus on these pressing issues.

ELIMINATION: NATIONAL INFRASTRUCTURE INVESTMENTS (TIGER)
Department of Transportation

The Budget proposes to eliminate funding for the unauthorized TIGER discretionary grant program, which awards grants to projects that are generally eligible for funding under existing surface transportation formula programs.

Funding Summary
(In millions of dollars)

	2017 CR	2018 Request	2018 Change from 2017
Budget Authority	499	0	-499

Justification

This program began as part of the 2009 stimulus bill and has not been authorized under the last two multi-year surface transportation authorization acts. It provides Federal funding for projects with localized benefits, and often these projects do not rise to the level of national or regional significance. Further, this program is similar to the Department of Transportation's Nationally Significant Freight and Highway Projects grant program, authorized by the FAST Act of 2015, which supports larger highway and multimodal freight projects with demonstrable national or regional benefits. The Nationally Significant Freight and Highway Projects grant program is authorized at an annual average of $900 million through 2020.

REDUCTION: COMMUNITY DEVELOPMENT FINANCIAL INSTITUTIONS FUND
Department of the Treasury

The Budget proposes to eliminate new grants to Community Development Financial Institutions (CDFIs), but requests $14 million for oversight of existing commitments and administration of the CDFI Fund's other programs. The CDFI industry has matured, and these institutions should have access to private capital needed to extend credit and provide financial services.

Funding Summary
(In millions of dollars)

	2017 CR	2018 Request	2018 Change from 2017
CDFI Fund Grants	210	0	-210
CDFI Fund Administration	24	14	-10
Total	234	14	-220

Justification

Created in 1994, but currently unauthorized, the CDFI Fund provides grants, loans, and tax credits to a national network of CDFIs to expand the availability of credit, investment capital, and financial services for low-income and underserved people and communities. Today, with nearly 1,100 Treasury-certified CDFIs, including loan funds, community development banks, credit unions, and venture capital funds active in all 50 states, that goal has been achieved. The Budget eliminates funding for the Fund's four discretionary grant and direct loan programs (i.e., the CDFI Program, the Bank Enterprise Awards Program, the Native American CDFI Assistance (NACA) program, and the Healthy Food Financing Initiative) targeted at this now mature industry. The Budget maintains funding for administrative expenses to support ongoing CDFI Fund program activities, including the New Markets Tax Credit program, and proposes to extend the CDFI Bond Guarantee Program, which offers CDFIs low-cost, long-term financing at no cost to taxpayers, as the program requires no credit subsidy.

ELIMINATION: GLOBAL AGRICULTURE AND FOOD SECURITY PROGRAM
Department of the Treasury

The Global Agriculture and Food Security Program (GAFSP) is a multi-donor trust fund that supports agricultural investment plans of poor countries. The United States has sufficient funding to meet its 2012 pledge to fund GAFSP. No new funding is required in 2018.

Funding Summary
(In millions of dollars)

	2017 CR	2018 Request	2018 Change from 2017
Budget Authority	43	0	-43

Justification

The 2012 pledge period is over. The United States contributed $475 million towards the initial GAFSP pledge in 2009. In 2012, the U.S. pledged to contribute $1 for every $2 dollars in new contributions from other donors over the announced period of the pledge, up to a maximum of $475 million. That period has ended, and the United States has sufficient prior-year funding to fulfill the pledge to match other donors' contributions.

Other donors' support of GAFSP has been limited. While other donors may continue to support GAFSP, their support for the 2012 pledge has been moderate at best. Since 2012, other donors' actual contributions totaled $342 million through 2016, and the United States contributed over $170 million in matching funds. Only 10 donors provided funding for GAFSP since its inception, contributing less than $1.7 billion in total, with the United States counting for 42 percent of the initial pledge and $645 million, or 40 percent, of all contributions since 2009.

The United States Government and other donors provide ample funding to support the same type of agricultural investments in poor countries through other mechanisms where there is evidence of impact and alignment with U.S. strategic priorities.

REDUCTION: SPECIAL INSPECTOR GENERAL FOR THE TROUBLED ASSET RELIEF PROGRAM
Department of the Treasury

The Budget reduces funding for the Special Inspector General for the Troubled Asset Relief Program (SIGTARP) by 50 percent, commensurate with the wind-down of TARP programs.

Funding Summary
(In millions of dollars)

	2017 CR	2018 Request	2018 Change from 2017
Budget Authority	41	20	-21

Justification

Funding for SIGTARP is reduced, reflecting that less than one percent of Treasury's TARP investments remain outstanding, nearly 80 percent of Housing Finance Agency Hardest Hit Funds have been disbursed, and the application periods for the Federal Housing Administration Refinance program and Making Home Affordable initiative have ended. SIGTARP will retain access to mandatory funding provided in previous years that will help the office manage an orderly wind-down of its operations.

REDUCTION: CORPS OF ENGINEERS - AGENCY TOPLINE
Corps of Engineers

The Budget for the Army Corps of Engineers civil works program (Corps) focuses on investments to maintain the performance of the key features of existing water resources infrastructure that the Corps owns and operates, and the navigation channels that serve the Nation's largest coastal ports. It also supports the construction of projects that would provide a high economic or environmental return to the Nation or that address a significant risk to public safety.

Funding Summary
(In millions of dollars)

	2017 CR	2018 Request	2018 Change from 2017
Budget Authority	5,978	5,002	-976

Justification

The Budget advances the three main missions of the Corps, which are commercial navigation, flood and storm damage reduction, and aquatic ecosystem restoration. It uses performance guidelines to ensure the best use of funds. The Budget gives priority to maintaining the performance of existing infrastructure over the construction of new projects. It provides $3.2 billion for the operation and maintenance program (including $142 million in the Mississippi River and tributaries account) and $1.1 billion for the construction program (including $110 million in the Mississippi River and tributaries account).

REDUCTION: CATEGORICAL GRANTS
Environmental Protection Agency

The Environmental Protection Agency (EPA) provides categorical grants to help fund State environmental program offices and activities. Many States have been delegated authority to implement and enforce Federal environmental laws including the Clean Air Act, Clean Water Act, and Safe Drinking Water Act. The Budget proposes to reduce many of these grants and eliminate others to better focus and prioritize environmental activities on core functions required by Federal environmental laws.

Funding Summary
(In millions of dollars)

	2017 CR	2018 Request	2018 Change from 2017
Budget Authority	1,079	597	-482

Justification

EPA categorical grant funding is intended to help States meet Federal environmental law requirements and standards. The Budget proposes to eliminate or substantially reduce Federal investment in State environmental activities that go beyond EPA's statutory requirements. States may be able to adjust to reduced funding levels by reducing or eliminating additional activities not required under Federal law, prioritizing programs, and seeking other funding sources including fees.

ELIMINATION: ENERGY STAR AND VOLUNTARY CLIMATE PROGRAMS
Environmental Protection Agency

The Budget eliminates funding for Energy Star and several other voluntary partnership programs related to energy and climate change. These programs are not essential to the Environmental Protection Agency's (EPA) core mission and can be implemented by the private sector.

Funding Summary
(In millions of dollars)

	2017 CR	2018 Request	2018 Change from 2017
Budget Authority	66	0	-66

Justification

The Administration is committed to returning EPA to its core work. There is no need for EPA to administer voluntary partnership and certification programs like Energy Star with taxpayer dollars, given the popularity and significant private benefits these programs provide to industry partners and consumers. Similar certification programs have been and continue to be successfully administered by non-governmental entities like industry associations and consumer groups.

REDUCTION: ENFORCEMENT
Environmental Protection Agency

The Budget proposes to reduce the Environmental Protection Agency's (EPA) environmental enforcement activities. The reduction to EPA's Office of Enforcement and Compliance Assurance programs will allow the agency to re-focus enforcement priorities on programs that are not delegated to States and avoid duplication of effort in States with delegated enforcement authority.

Funding Summary
(In millions of dollars)

	2017 CR	2018 Request	2018 Change from 2017
Budget Authority	548	419	-129

Justification

Environmental enforcement is a shared effort between the Federal government and States to achieve a cleaner and healthier Nation. Many environmental laws authorize this cooperative arrangement, where States may be delegated authority to implement Federal environmental laws and the EPA serves in an oversight role. The Budget allows the agency to maintain a core enforcement oversight role to ensure a consistent and effective program, but eliminates duplication of enforcement actions carried out by the States, and focuses Federal enforcement efforts in those States that do not have delegated authority.

ELIMINATION: GEOGRAPHIC PROGRAMS
Environmental Protection Agency

Geographic Programs fund a variety of ecosystem protection activities within specific watersheds, including the Great Lakes, Chesapeake Bay, Puget Sound, and others. These activities are primarily local efforts and the responsibility for coordinating and funding these efforts generally belongs with States and local partnerships.

Funding Summary
(In millions of dollars)

	2017 CR	2018 Request	2018 Change from 2017
Budget Authority	427	0	-427

Justification

Eliminating the Environmental Protection Agency's Geographic programs refocuses the agency on core national work. These programs perform local ecosystem protection and restoration activities, which are best handled by local and State entities. The Geographic Programs, including the Great Lakes Restoration Initiative and the Chesapeake Bay Program, have received significant federal funding, coordination, and oversight to date. State and local groups are engaged and capable of taking on management of clean-up and restoration of these water bodies.

REDUCTION: RESEARCH AND DEVELOPMENT
Environmental Protection Agency

The Budget reconfigures and restructures the Environmental Protection Agency's (EPA) activities in research and development to focus on research objectives that support statutory requirements. Extramural Science to Achieve Results (STAR) grants will not receive funding.

Funding Summary
(In millions of dollars)

	2017 CR	2018 Request	2018 Change from 2017
Budget Authority	483	249	-234

Justification

As EPA shifts its programmatic resources to focus on core Agency responsibilities, the scientific research and development activities will also be reconfigured and restructured. At lower funding levels for the Office of Research and Development, the Agency would prioritize intramural research activities that are either related to statutory requirements or that support basic and early stage research and development activities in the environmental and human health sciences.

REDUCTION: SUPERFUND
Environmental Protection Agency

The Budget proposes to reduce funding for the Environmental Protection Agency's (EPA) Hazardous Substance Superfund Account, focusing on reining in Superfund administrative costs and promoting efficiencies. The Budget proposes that EPA would optimize the use of existing settlement funds for sites where those funds exist and will look for ways to remove some of the barriers that have delayed the program's ability to return sites to the community.

Funding Summary
(In millions of dollars)

	2017 CR	2018 Request	2018 Change from 2017
Budget Authority	1,092	762	-330

Justification

The Hazardous Substance Superfund Account funds the EPA's efforts to address the emergency release of hazardous substances and the long-term cleanup of hazardous waste sites. The EPA relies on a combination of appropriated funds and settlements with responsible parties to perform its duties. There are 1,337 active sites on the National Priorities List (NPL) of the most hazardous sites in the nation, many of which have been on the NPL for decades. While a good portion of these sites include complex groundwater, soil, and sediment contamination, some are viewed as languishing since the indirect costs of administration have gone up. This Budget challenges the EPA to identify efficiencies in administrative costs and optimize the use of settlement funds for the cleanup actions at sites where those funds are available. The Budget provides the opportunity for the agency to identify what barriers have been preventing sites from returning to communities and design solutions to overcome those barriers.

ELIMINATION: FIVE EARTH SCIENCE MISSIONS
National Aeronautics and Space Administration

Due to competing priorities within the National Aeronautics and Space Administration (NASA) Science program, the Budget proposes to terminate five Earth Science Missions: Radiation Budget Instrument (RBI), PACE, OCO-3, DSCOVR Earth-viewing instruments, CLARREO Pathfinder.

Funding Summary
(In millions of dollars)

	2017 CR	2018 Request	2018 Change from 2017
Budget Authority	191	0	-191

Justification

The missions proposed for termination are lower-priority science missions that cannot be accommodated under constrained budgets. The proposed termination of these five missions restructures the NASA Earth science portfolio within the available budget in a way that causes the least impact to NASA's ability to execute a balanced, comprehensive Earth science program that meets the highest priorities of the science community.

The RBI would have flown on a future weather satellite to make measurements of the Earth's reflected sunlight and emitted thermal radiation. Similar instruments flying now and planned for near-term launch will continue to provide continuity for the data record. Additionally, the instrument has experienced cost growth and technical challenges, as technological innovations for RBI have proven more difficult than anticipated to implement.

DSCOVR, OCO-3, and PACE were not identified as high-priority NASA missions in the previous Earth Science Decadal Survey, which reflects the science community's consensus views on Earth science space-borne priorities. The DSCOVR Earth-viewing instruments (currently in space) provide images of the sunlit side of the Earth and measure the energy reflected and emitted from it. These instruments do not contribute to the core DSCOVR mission of providing measurements for space weather. OCO-3 would have investigated the distribution of carbon dioxide on Earth. These measurements are currently being taken by NASA's OCO-2 mission, and future measurements are planned by other nations. The PACE mission would have provided atmospheric aerosol measurements and ocean color measurements, some of which are being provided by existing U.S. and European satellites.

The CLARREO Pathfinder mission would have demonstrated measurement technologies for a larger, more expensive, potential future mission focused on improving detection of climate trends. This demonstration mission is in the earliest stages of implementation and is eliminated to achieve cost savings.

ELIMINATION: OFFICE OF EDUCATION
National Aeronautics and Space Administration

The Budget terminates National Aeronautics and Space Administration's (NASA) Office of Education, which has experienced significant challenges in implementing a focused NASA-wide education strategy.

Funding Summary
(In millions of dollars)

	2017 CR	2018 Request	2018 Change from 2017
Budget Authority	115	37	-78

Justification

The Office of Education has experienced significant challenges in implementing a focused NASA-wide education strategy, including challenges in providing oversight and integration of Agency-wide education activities. Comprehensive evaluations of major programs have not been conducted. Additionally, while output data (e.g., number of people funded, number of papers generated, number of events supported) has been tracked, outcome-related data demonstrating program effectiveness has been insufficient to assess the impact of the overall Office of Education portfolio. Given these challenges and current fiscal constraints, the Budget proposes to terminate this office and proposes $37 million for close-out costs.

REDUCTION: NATIONAL SCIENCE FOUNDATION, RESEARCH AND RELATED ACTIVITIES AND EDUCATION GRANTS
National Science Foundation

The Budget proposes a reduction of 11 percent to National Science Foundation (NSF) grant programs. The Congress authorized establishment of the NSF in 1950 "to promote the progress of science; to advance the national health, prosperity, and welfare; to secure the national defense..." NSF is the funding source for approximately 24 percent of all federally supported basic research conducted by America's colleges and universities.

Funding Summary
(In millions of dollars)

	2017 CR	2018 Request	2018 Change from 2017
Budget Authority	6,900	6,124	-776

Justification

The reduction in NSF funding aligns with the Administration's goal to transfer funds across agencies in order to strengthen national security and public safety. Under this proposal, NSF will focus on new opportunities to position our Nation at the cutting edge of global science and engineering leadership and to invest in basic research that advances U.S. prosperity, security, health, and well-being. Through this proposal, NSF continues to invest in research infrastructure to enable transformative discoveries. The Budget proposes cuts to several programs that were increased during the last Administration, including funding for Clean Energy R&D, the Ocean Observatories Initiative, and Innovations at the Nexus of Food, Energy, and Water Services to focus on NSF's core research programs.

ELIMINATION: CHEMICAL SAFETY BOARD
Other Independent Agencies

The U.S. Chemical Safety and Hazard Investigation Board (CSB) is proposed for elimination consistent with the Administration's efforts to close programs that are largely duplicative of other Agency efforts.

Funding Summary
(In millions of dollars)

	2017 CR	2018 Request	2018 Change from 2017
Budget Authority	11	9	-2

Justification

CSB is an independent agency authorized by the Clean Air Act Amendments of 1990, whose mission is to investigate accidents at chemical facilities to determine the conditions or circumstances that led to the accident. Congress intended CSB to be an investigative arm that is wholly independent of the rulemaking, inspection, and enforcement authorities of its partner agencies in making recommendations on actions that can be taken to prevent similar accidents from occurring in the future. While CSB has done some outstanding work on its investigations, more often than not, its overlap with other agency investigative authorities has generated unhelpful friction. In recent years, CSB's recommendations have also been focused on the need for greater regulation of industry, which has frustrated both regulators and industry. The pressure to tie investigations to management priorities culminated in whistleblower complaints that led to critical reports issued by both the Environmental Protection Agency Office of the Inspector General and the U.S. House of Representatives Oversight and Government Reform Committee. While CSB's new leadership is making progress on the previous management challenges, due to the duplicative nature of its work, the Budget recommends eliminating the agency.

ELIMINATION: CORPORATION FOR NATIONAL AND COMMUNITY SERVICE
Other Independent Agencies

The Budget proposes to eliminate the Corporation for National and Community Service (CNCS) and to provide funding for the orderly shutdown of the Agency. Funding community service and subsidizing the operation of nonprofit organizations is outside the role of the Federal Government. To the extent these activities have value, they should be supported by the nonprofit and private sectors and not with Federal subsidies provided through the complex Federal grant structure run by CNCS.

Funding Summary
(In millions of dollars)

	2017 CR	2018 Request	2018 Change from 2017
Budget Authority	1,093	135	-958

Justification

CNCS is a grant-making agency that funds service opportunities, promotes volunteering, and helps nonprofit organizations engage volunteers. Members funded through CNCS grants typically receive a living allowance and education award of over $5,000 for their service. While some of the programs supported by CNCS grants have demonstrated effectiveness, and CNCS has made progress in evaluating its programs, some of the Agency's programs struggle to measure and demonstrate their impact. In addition, the agency has struggled to effectively implement complex program requirements and has faced significant management challenges.

Funding community service and subsidizing the operation of non-profit organizations is outside the proper role of the Federal Government. Over 60 million Americans perform volunteer activities in their communities each year absent subsidies from the Federal Government, and would likely continue to do so after CNCS is eliminated.[1] Programs currently funded by CNCS that demonstrate value should be able to compete successfully for funding from individual donors and the nonprofit and private sectors.

Citations

[1] Bureau of Labor Statistics: *Volunteering in the United States – 2015*, USDL-16-0363, (February 2016).

ELIMINATION: CORPORATION FOR PUBLIC BROADCASTING
Other Independent Agencies

The Budget proposes to eliminate Federal funding for the Corporation for Public Broadcasting (CPB). CPB grants represent a small share of the total funding for the Public Broadcasting Service (PBS) and National Public Radio (NPR), which primarily rely on private donations to fund their operations. To conduct an orderly closeout of Federal funding, the Budget requests $30 million, which includes funding for personnel costs of $16.2 million, rental costs of $8.9 million, and other costs totaling $5.4 million.

Funding Summary
(In millions of dollars)

	2017 CR	2018 Request	2018 Change from 2017
Budget Authority	484	30	-454

Justification

CPB provides grants to qualified public television and radio stations to be used at their discretion for purposes related to program production or acquisition, as well as for general operations. CPB also supports the production and acquisition of radio and television programs for national distribution. CPB funding comprises about 15 percent of the total amount spent on public broadcasting, with the remainder coming from non-Federal sources, with many large stations raising an even greater share. This private fundraising has proven durable, negating the need for continued Federal subsidies. Services such as PBS and NPR, which receive funding from the CPB, could make up the shortfall by increasing revenues from corporate sponsors, foundations, and members. In addition, alternatives to PBS and NPR programming have grown substantially since CPB was first established in 1967, greatly reducing the need for publicly funded programming options.

ELIMINATION: INSTITUTE OF MUSEUM AND LIBRARY SERVICES
Other Independent Agencies

The Budget proposes eliminating the Institute of Museum and Library Services (IMLS), which provides funding to museums and libraries across the country through formula and competitive grant awards. IMLS's funding supplements local, State, and private funds, which provide the vast majority of funding to museums and libraries.

Funding Summary
(In millions of dollars)

	2017 CR	2018 Request	2018 Change from 2017
Budget Authority	230	23	-207

Justification

IMLS provides funding to museums and libraries across the country through formula and competitive grant awards. IMLS provides $156 million in formula funds to State Library Administrative Agencies and administers several smaller competitive grant programs for libraries and museums that fund activities such as scholarships for librarian training and digital resources to support educational, employment, and other training opportunities. IMLS's funding supplements local, State, and private funds, which provide the vast majority of funding to museums and libraries. Furthermore, given that IMLS primarily supports discrete, short-term projects as opposed to operation-sustaining funds, it is unlikely the elimination of IMLS would result in the closure of a significant number of libraries and museums.

ELIMINATION: INTERNATIONAL DEVELOPMENT FOUNDATIONS
Other Independent Agencies

The Budget proposes to eliminate the African Development Foundation (ADF) and the Inter-American Foundation (IAF) in order to streamline functions across Government. The funding included in the Budget reflects close-out costs for ADF and IAF, particularly to pay severance costs. No additional Federal funding will be needed in 2019 or beyond. The eliminations reflect the Administration's interest in maintaining overall discretionary fiscal discipline in a manner that emphasizes domestic needs over foreign assistance spending.

Funding Summary
(In millions of dollars)

	2017 CR	2018 Request	2018 Change from 2017
African Development Foundation	30	8	-22
Inter-American Foundation	22	5	-17

Justification

ADF and IAF were first authorized over 30 years ago, but have both operated without an authorization since 1987. ADF and IAF serve niche missions providing small grants to African-owned and led enterprises (in the case of ADF) and to grassroots organizations in Latin America and the Caribbean (in the case of IAF), which are not critical to U.S. foreign policy and are potentially duplicative of other efforts in the non-profit and private sectors. While labeled as foundations, these organizations are actually Federal agencies that are among a panoply of duplicative development efforts funded by the Federal Government. For example, the United States also supports development assistance to both regions through the United States Agency for International Development, the Millennium Challenge Corporation, the African Development Bank, the Inter-American Development Bank, and the World Bank. In order to better concentrate funds for top development priorities and utilize scalable mechanisms to achieve significant impact, the Budget proposes eliminating Federal funding for both ADF and IAF.

ELIMINATION: LEGAL SERVICES CORPORATION
Other Independent Agencies

The Budget seeks to end the one-size-fits-all model of providing legal services through a single Federal grant program, the Legal Services Corporation (LSC). This proposed elimination puts more control in the hands of State and local governments which better understand the needs of their communities.

Funding Summary
(In millions of dollars)

	2017 CR	2018 Request	2018 Change from 2017
Budget Authority	384	33	-351

Justification

This proposed elimination will encourage nonprofit organizations, businesses, law firms, and religious institutions to develop new models for providing legal aid, such as pro bono work, law school clinics, and innovative technologies. The proposal also puts more control in the hands of State and local governments which better understand the needs of their communities. Further, the LSC is not subject to the same accountability measures as other agencies, such as the Antideficiency Act and certain public reporting requirements. The LSC's indefinite appropriation authorization expired in 1980.

ELIMINATION: NATIONAL ENDOWMENT FOR THE ARTS
Other Independent Agencies

The Budget proposes to begin shutting down the National Endowment for the Arts (NEA) in 2018, given the notable funding support provided by private and other public sources and because the Administration does not consider NEA activities to be core Federal responsibilities.

Funding Summary
(In millions of dollars)

	2017 CR	2018 Request	2018 Change from 2017
Budget Authority	148	29	-119

Justification

Established in 1965, the NEA uses partnerships with State arts agencies, other Federal agencies, and the philanthropic sector, to support arts learning, cultural heritage, and increasing access to the arts across the country. Forty percent of NEA funding is provided directly to State arts councils, with the remaining distributed as grants to theaters, libraries, schools, and non-profit organizations.

In 2014, NEA funding represented just four percent of total public and private support for the arts in the United States.

ELIMINATION: NATIONAL ENDOWMENT FOR THE HUMANITIES
Other Independent Agencies

The Budget proposes to begin shutting down the National Endowment for the Humanities (NEH) in 2018, given the other sources of funding for humanities and because the Administration does not consider the activities within this agency to be core Federal responsibilities.

Funding Summary
(In millions of dollars)

	2017 CR	2018 Request	2018 Change from 2017
Budget Authority	148	42	-106

Justification

Established in 1965, the NEH is intended to "serve and strengthen our Republic by promoting excellence in the humanities and conveying the lessons of history to all Americans." Nearly 33 percent of NEH funding is provided directly to State humanities councils, with the remaining distributed as grants to individuals, universities, libraries, museums, and schools.

Beyond Federal support, additional funding for humanities in the United States comes from private donations from individuals, corporations, and foundations.

ELIMINATION: NEIGHBORHOOD REINVESTMENT CORPORATION
Other Independent Agencies

The Budget proposes to end Federal support for the Neighborhood Reinvestment Corporation (NRC), commonly known as NeighborWorks, a statutorily chartered non-profit that receives the vast majority of its funding from Federal funds. A strong return on these funds has not been documented.

Funding Summary
(In millions of dollars)

	2017 CR	2018 Request	2018 Change from 2017
Budget Authority	175	27	-148

Justification

NRC supports a network of local housing and community development organizations through grants, managerial oversight, and training. NRC is not a unique provider of housing and community services, and has been unable to document with evaluative rigor that its Federal funding leads to higher performance or better outcomes compared to the work of similar organizations. NRC's performance measurement system is largely a collection of output indicators rather than strong housing and community development outcomes. The production that members of the NRC network achieve comes largely from financial sources other than NRC.[1] Further, NRC has been unable to produce rigorous statistical evidence to link the provision of NRC's funding and technical support with improved outcomes.

The last year that NRC had an authorization for appropriations was 1994.

Citations

[1] Less than 2 percent of the network's investments come from NRC's Federal funds. NeighborWorks: *Community Report*, http://www.neighborworks.org/About-Us/Community-Report, (retrieved May 8, 2017).

ELIMINATION: OVERSEAS PRIVATE INVESTMENT CORPORATION
Other Independent Agencies

The Budget proposes ceasing new business operations and initiating the wind-down of the Overseas Private Investment Corporation (OPIC) starting in 2018 to reduce unnecessary Federal interventions that distort the free market. The wind-down of OPIC is also consistent with the President's commitment to focus less overseas and more domestically, and will achieve savings in OPIC's administrative and subsidy expenses. In addition to the Budget request for $61 million in budget authority to support wind-down costs, OPIC will also collect $367 million in offsetting collections from loans, loan guarantees, and risk insurance activities executed in 2017 and prior years.

Funding Summary
(In millions of dollars)

	2017 CR	2018 Request	2018 Change from 2017
Budget Authority: Administrative Expenses and Subsidy	83	61	-22
Memo: Offsetting Collections [Non-Add]	-519	-367	152

Justification

OPIC, which provides financing and political risk insurance to help American businesses invest in emerging markets, is not currently authorized beyond 2017. Development Finance Institutions (DFIs) like OPIC can at times displace the private sector, particularly in emerging and developing markets that have active international finance firms or domestic financial institutions capable of providing similar financing. While the Administration wants U.S. businesses to invest in emerging markets to grow their businesses and create American jobs, private sector financing is often available.

OPIC has not had a stand-alone authorization bill since 2008; instead, Congress has extended OPIC's authorization annually via appropriations. This has allowed OPIC to operate for nearly 10 years without any changes by its authorizers, avoiding significant reforms that may have addressed some of these challenges while OPIC's portfolio continued to expand.

Due to OPIC's outstanding $22 billion portfolio and the long-term nature of some OPIC transactions, OPIC cannot be eliminated immediately without putting taxpayer dollars at risk. While the Budget would not support any new OPIC transactions starting in 2018, the Budget would support significantly reduced OPIC staff to monitor and maintain OPIC's existing portfolio, allowing for repayments to be collected and minimizing the risk to the taxpayer from OPIC's outstanding exposure.

ELIMINATION: REGIONAL COMMISSIONS
Other Independent Agencies

The Budget proposes to eliminate the Appalachian Regional Commission, the Delta Regional Authority, the Denali Commission, and the Northern Border Regional Commission, providing funding only for the orderly closure of the Agencies. The Budget restores control over community and economic development efforts to State and local governments and private entities.

Funding Summary
(In millions of dollars)

	2017 CR	2018 Request	2018 Change from 2017
Appalachian Regional Commission	146	27	-119
Delta Regional Authority	25	3	-22
Denali Commission	15	7	-8
Northern Border Regional Commission	8	1	-7

Justification

The Appalachian Regional Commission (ARC), the Delta Regional Authority (DRA), the Denali Commission and the Northern Border Regional Commission (NBRC) are independent agencies that award Federal grants for regional development. The proposed elimination of the regional commissions reflects the need to reduce unnecessary Federal spending and streamline the Federal Government's role, while encouraging States and localities to partner with the private sector to develop locally-tailored solutions to local problems.

In addition, the value or efficacy of certain regional commissions is undermined by the following: 1) A Government Accountability Office report issued over 30 years after the ARC's inception was unable to find any studies establishing a strong causal link between ARC grants and overall positive economic impact;[1] 2) The rationale for a unique and additional Federal subsidy to Alaska is difficult to justify given that the State of Alaska's oil revenues allow it to pay an annual dividend ($1,022 in 2016) to each of its residents;[2] 3) NBRC member States have declined to contribute their share of funding for the Commission's operating expenses, despite a statutory requirement to do so, established by the Congress as part of the Agency's operating structure.[3,4]

Citations

[1] Government Accountability Office: *Economic Development: Limited Information Exists on the Impact of Assistance Provided by Three Agencies*, GAO-RCED-96-103, (April 1996).

[2] State of Alaska Department of Revenue: *Permanent Fund Dividend Division, Annual Report 2016*, (2016).

[3] Northern Border Regional Commission: *2016 Annual Report*, Financial Statements, p. 34, (2016).

[4] 40 U.S.C. 15304(c).

ELIMINATION: U.S INSTITUTE OF PEACE
Other Independent Agencies

The Budget proposes to eliminate earmarked Federal funding for the United States Institute of Peace (USIP), given it serves a niche mission that duplicates other Federal programs. The funding included in the Budget reflects close-out costs for USIP, particularly to pay severance costs. No additional Federal funding will be needed in 2019 or beyond.

Funding Summary
(In millions of dollars)

	2017 CR	2018 Request	2018 Change from 2017
Budget Authority	35	19	-16

Justification

Congress created USIP as an independent, non-profit corporation in 1984, but USIP's authorization for appropriations expired in 2015. Even with an authorization, it is highly unusual for an independent organization to receive a direct appropriation without Executive Branch oversight. The Administration is seeking to end funding for organizations that may effectively serve niche missions, but which are not critical to the conduct of U.S. foreign policy, and which duplicate the efforts of other Federal programs or the non-profit and private sectors. Consistent with these efforts to streamline functions and close programs across Government, the Budget proposes to eliminate Federal funding for USIP.

ELIMINATION: U.S. TRADE AND DEVELOPMENT AGENCY
Other Independent Agencies

The Budget proposes to eliminate funding for the U.S. Trade and Development Agency (TDA), given its mission is more appropriately served by the private sector. The Administration's request of $12 million will allow TDA to conduct an orderly closeout of the agency beginning in 2018, which includes sufficient funding for personnel, rent, program, and other closeout costs. No additional funding will be needed in 2019 and beyond.

Funding Summary
(In millions of dollars)

	2017 CR	2018 Request	2018 Change from 2017
Budget Authority	60	12	-48

Justification

TDA's dual mission is to support U.S. exports and jobs, while advancing infrastructure development in developing and middle-income countries. Its main programmatic focus is to support U.S. private sector participation in infrastructure projects in middle-income countries. However, many of these projects would likely proceed without TDA support and could thus be supported by the private sector without Government involvement. While the Administration wants U.S. businesses to invest in emerging markets to grow their businesses and create American jobs, these businesses have incentive to invest and should rely on private sector financing. In general, the United States should not provide taxpayer subsidies except in rare situations, such as when limited support is needed to offset inappropriate subsidies that disadvantage U.S. businesses. In fact, supporting select U.S. businesses over others puts the Government in the business of picking winners and losers, potentially distorting the free market.

ELIMINATION: WOODROW WILSON INTERNATIONAL CENTER FOR SCHOLARS
Other Independent Agencies

The Budget proposes to eliminate activities supported through Federal appropriations at the Woodrow Wilson International Center for Scholars (Center), given these activities can be supported through private fundraising and the Administration does not consider them to be core Federal responsibilities. To conduct an orderly closeout of federally funded operations, the Budget requests $7.5 million in 2018.

Funding Summary
(In millions of dollars)

	2017 CR	2018 Request	2018 Change from 2017
Budget Authority	11	7	-4

Justification

The Center's mission is to be a nonpartisan policy forum and independent research institute for tackling global issues, and serves as the official living memorial for President Woodrow Wilson. Federal appropriations represent approximately one-third of total funding for the Center, which primarily relies on private donations for operations.

As a "living memorial," the Center works to achieve its mission by serving as a non-partisan policy forum, conducting independent research, and providing open dialogue for informing the policy community. This is achieved, in part, by hosting over 120 fellows from around the world each year who, along with staff, conduct research on policy issues confronting the United States, host public meetings and events, and undertake a wide-range of outreach activities.

ELIMINATE ALLOCATIONS TO THE HOUSING TRUST FUND AND CAPITAL MAGNET FUND
Multi-Agency

The Budget proposes to eliminate funding for the Housing Trust Fund and Capital Magnet Fund, two programs that provide Federal funding for affordable low-income housing. The Budget recognizes a greater role for State and local governments and the private sector in addressing affordable housing needs.

Funding Summary
(In millions of dollars)

	2018	2019	2020	2021	2022	2023	2024	2025	2026	2027	2018-22	2018-27
Proposed Change from Current Law..................	-194	-104	-177	-247	-321	-335	-348	-367	-375	-378	-1,043	-2,846

Justification

The Housing Trust Fund, managed by the Department of Housing and Urban Development, provides grants to States to increase and preserve the supply of affordable housing primarily for extremely low-income families. The Capital Magnet Fund, managed by the Department of the Treasury's Community Development Financial Institutions (CDFI) Fund, provides grants to CDFIs and nonprofit housing organizations that are leveraged to finance affordable housing and related economic development activities. Originally established by the Housing and Economic Recovery Act of 2008 with dedicated funding from Fannie Mae and Freddie Mac assessments, a total of $627 million has been allocated to the funds since 2016.

Housing for low-income families is currently funded by multiple funding sources, including Federal, State, and local governments, as well as the private and nonprofit sectors. The result is a fragmented system with varying rules and regulations that create overlap and inefficiencies, as well as challenges to measuring collective performance.[1] The Budget would devolve some affordable housing activities to State and local governments who are better positioned to comprehensively address the array of unique market challenges, local policies, and impediments that lead to housing affordability problems.

Citations

[1] Government Accountability Office: *Affordable Rental Housing: Assistance Is Provided by Federal, State, and Local Programs, but There Is Incomplete Information on Collective Performance.* GAO-15-645, (September 2015).

REDUCE IMPROPER PAYMENTS AND OTHER PROGRAM INTEGRITY
Multi-Agency

By 2027, the Budget proposes to curtail Government-wide improper payments by half through actions to improve payment accuracy and tighten administrative controls.

Funding Summary
(In millions of dollars)

	2018	2019	2020	2021	2022	2023	2024	2025	2026	2027	2018-22	2018-27
Reduce Improper Payments Government-wide..................	0	-719	-1,482	-2,383	-4,288	-4,549	-9,652	-20,480	-38,024	-57,633	-8,872	-139,210
OTHER PROGRAM INTEGRITY, TOTAL...............	-167	-469	-1,005	-1,064	-1,061	-962	-1,034	-1,151	-1,186	-1,225	-3,766	-9,324
Unemployment Insurance Program Integrity Package.....................	-94	-215	-251	-249	-243	-211	-253	-249	-241	-228	-1,052	-2,234
Reemployment Services and Eligibility Assessments..........	0	-88	-541	-562	-522	-411	-413	-493	-499	-519	-1,713	-4,048
Increase oversight of paid tax return preparers.....................	-14	-31	-35	-38	-42	-47	-50	-55	-61	-66	-160	-439
Provide more flexible authority for the IRS to address correctable errors..................	-30	-61	-64	-65	-67	-70	-71	-74	-76	-77	-287	-655
Hold Fraud Facilitators Liable for Overpayments.................	0	0	-1	-1	-1	-1	-1	-1	-1	-1	-3	-8
Government Wide Use of CBP Entry/Exit Data to Prevent Improper Payment.................	0	0	-1	-5	-11	-20	-26	-31	-40	-43	-17	-177
Allow SSA to Use Commercial Databases to Verify Real Property Data in the SSI Program........................	-12	-28	-44	-53	-60	-69	-70	-68	-76	-79	-197	-559
Increase the Overpayment Collection Threshold for OASDI..................................	-8	-26	-43	-59	-77	-93	-107	-135	-144	-156	-213	-848
Authorize SSA to Use All Collection Tools to Recover Funds in Certain Scenarios............................	0	-2	-2	-3	-4	-4	-5	-5	-5	-11	-11	-41
Exclude SSA debts from discharge in bankruptcy.........	-9	-18	-23	-29	-34	-36	-38	-40	-43	-45	-113	-315

Justification

The estimated Government-wide improper payment rate and dollar amount are intolerable. In 2016, the improper payment dollar estimate reached an all-time high of $144 billion and a rate of 4.67 percent. Even though 95 percent of all Federal Government payments are made properly, any waste of taxpayer money is unacceptable. As a steward of taxpayer dollars, it is the responsibility of the United States Government to execute its financial transactions in an efficient and prudent manner. Central to this is a particular focus on preventing and reducing improper payments and fraud.

An improper payment is any payment that was made to the wrong person, at the wrong time, or for the wrong amount, potentially resulting in a monetary loss to the Government. Generally, improper payments are caused by administrative or processing errors, the inability to authenticate recipient eligibility, or insufficient documentation to determine whether the payment was proper. Improper payments may be the result of fraud when one party intentionally makes a false claim to receive a Government benefit.

For the past few years, both the amount of improper payments reported and the rate have been rising. At the same time, Agencies have been recovering approximately $20 billion in overpayments through payment recapture audits and other methods.

Although approximately 120 programs contributed to the Government-wide improper payment estimation in 2016, five programs account for approximately 80 percent of the Government-wide estimate. Executive Branch Agencies have ongoing interactions with their Inspectors General and the Government Accountability Office to improve payment integrity, with a specific focus on these five programs.

While some of the increase in improper payment can be attributed to improved reporting, the Budget proposes savings associated with the President's promise to crack down on improper payments. There is compelling evidence that investments in administrative resources can significantly decrease the rate of improper payments and recoup many times their initial investment.

The Budget proposes to make significant investments in activities that ensure that taxpayer dollars are spent for purposes for which they were intended. By 2027, the Budget proposes to reduce Government-wide improper payments by half through actions to improve payment accuracy and tighten administrative controls.

It is important to keep in mind that not all improper payments are fraudulent or represent a loss to the Government. The Budget prioritizes reducing the amount of improper payments that represent cash out the door. Addressing these types of improper payments is a central component of the Administration's overall efforts to eliminate waste, fraud, and abuse and cut the improper payment in half by 2027.

Combating improper payments within the Federal Government is a top priority for this Administration. This Administration will explore new and groundbreaking ways to address the problem. Additional program integrity and improper payment proposals are found in the Budget Process chapter in the *Analytical Perspectives* volume.

REFORM FEDERAL DISABILITY PROGRAMS
Multi-Agency

The Budget proposes to evaluate creative and effective ways to promote greater labor force participation (LFP) of people with disabilities by expanding demonstration authority that allows the Administration to test new program rules and requires mandatory participation by program applicants and beneficiaries. An expert panel will identify specific changes to program rules that would increase LFP and reduce program participation, informed by successful demonstration results and other evidence. This reform proposal is accompanied by other smaller reforms to address inequities in the system and close loopholes that make the program more susceptible to fraud.

Funding Summary
(In millions of dollars)

	2018	2019	2020	2021	2022	2023	2024	2025	2026	2027	2018-22	2018-27
Test new approaches and reform Disability Programs.....	100	100	100	100	100	-2,494	-5,069	-9,332	-13,809	-18,627	500	-48,831
Reduce 12 month retroactive DI benefits to 6 months..........	-113	-643	-797	-951	-1,043	-1,112	-1,191	-1,272	-1,349	-1,430	-3,547	-9,901
Create sliding scale for multi-recipient SSI families.....	-743	-827	-861	-882	-956	-906	-862	-955	-979	-1,002	-4,269	-8,973
Offset overlapping unemployment and disability payments...............................	0	-58	-249	-329	-324	-319	-323	-323	-296	-317	-960	-2,538
Reinstate the reconsideration review stage in 10 states.......	0	71	-10	-59	-526	-246	-263	-305	-354	-376	-524	-2,068
Eliminate Workers Compensation Reverse Offset.................................	0	-3	-8	-12	-16	-19	-22	-25	-28	-31	-39	-164
Create a probationary period for Administrative Law Judges (ALJs)................................	0	0	0	0	0	0	0	0	0	0	0	0
Total..	-756	-1,360	-1,825	-2,133	-2,765	-5,096	-7,730	-12,212	-16,815	-21,783	-8,839	-72,475

Justification

Reform Disability Programs. Currently, people with disabilities have low rates of LFP-20 percent-which is less than a third of the LFP rate of the overall working age population. There is a common expectation that receipt of disability insurance benefits results in a permanent exit from the labor force. The Budget challenges this assumption by evaluating alternative program designs that will help individuals with disabilities remain attached to the labor force and individuals with temporary work disabilities return-to-work.

As part of this reform effort, the Administration would call on the Congress to establish an expert panel that would identify specific changes to program rules that increase LFP and reduce participation on disability programs based on the results of successful demonstrations and other evidence. This panel would be responsible for making recommendations to reduce participation levels that would be directly tied to reaching a 5 percent reduction in Disability Insurance (DI) and Supplemental Security Income (SSI) projected outlays by 2027.

To maximize the potential of success, the Administration would simultaneously test a variety of strategies. The Administration is calling on the Congress to mandate participation by applicants and program beneficiaries in these projects including:

1) Test "time limited benefits" for beneficiaries for a period when they would be more likely to return to work;

2) Require applicants to engage in job-seeking activities before their application is considered;

3) Push existing State vocational rehabilitation offices to intervene earlier with individuals on a track to end up on DI;

4) Replicate welfare-to-work strategies in State TANF offices to provide wellness care and vocational services to welfare applicants that cannot work due to a short-term or uncontrolled health condition; and

5) Mandate that lower back pain and arthritis sufferers engage in rehabilitation traditionally used in occupational health treatment services before receiving benefits.

On a separate track, the Office of Disability Employment Policy (ODEP) at the Department of Labor would lead the implementation of a demonstration project to test the effectiveness of Washington State's Centers of Occupational Health and Education (COHE) program to improve labor force participation and attachment of individuals with temporary injuries and disabilities. While COHE is focused on workers' compensation related injuries, the demonstration will test the effects of implementing key features of the model in other States or municipalities, and/or for a broader population beyond workers' compensation. Some of the key features include care and service coordination, population screening and monitoring, increased access and targeted vocational rehabilitation and work supports, workplace accommodations, and technical assistance to healthcare providers and employers.

Reduce 12 month retroactive DI benefits to six months. New DI beneficiaries are eligible for up to 12 months of benefits before the date of their application, depending upon the date they became disabled. This proposal would reduce retroactivity for disabled workers, which is the same policy already in effect for individuals receiving retirement benefits. This proposal will not modify retroactivity for Medicare eligibility.

Create sliding scale for multi-recipient SSI families. Currently, families receive an equal amount for each SSI child recipient. However, economies of scale in some types of consumption —housing, in particular— reduces per capita living expenses and therefore means that two children generally do not need twice the income as one child. Federal poverty guidelines and other means-tested benefits take into account these efficiencies. The Budget proposes to create a sliding scale for SSI disability benefits that considers the number of additional family recipients. It would keep the maximum benefit for one recipient the same as in current law but reduce benefits for additional recipients in the same family.

Offset overlapping unemployment and disability payments. The Budget proposes to close a loophole that allows individuals to receive Unemployment Insurance (UI) and DI for the same period of joblessness. The proposal would offset the DI benefit to account for concurrent receipt of UI benefits. Under current law, concurrent receipt of DI benefits and unemployment compensation is allowable. UI is intended to compensate individuals for short-term bouts of unemployment while they look to return to work while DI is intended to compensate individuals who cannot return to work on a long-term basis due to a disability, allowing double dipping that is unnecessary and wasteful.

Reinstate the reconsideration review application stage in 10 States. The Budget proposes reinstating reconsideration in 10 States, conforming these States with the practices used in the rest of the Nation. This reform requires a second review by the State Disability Determination Services (DDS) before an appeal goes to an Administrative Law Judge (ALJ). Other States already require disability applicants to have their claim "reconsidered" before they can appeal to an ALJ.

Eliminate Workers' Compensation (WC) Reverse Offset. The Budget proposes to eliminate reverse offsets in 15 States where WC benefits are offset instead of DI benefits. Currently, in most States, the combination of benefits from WC and DI is limited to 80 percent of the recipient's earnings before they were disabled. If necessary, DI benefits are usually offset to meet the limit. However, 15 States currently reduce the benefit from WC rather than DI in order to achieve the 80 percent limit, creating an unjustified inequity across States. This option would eliminate the reverse offsets in these States.

Create a probationary period for Administrative Law Judges. The Budget proposes to create a probationary period for ALJs. This option would create a one-year probationary period, similar to the Senior

Executive Service, to ensure an ALJ is performing at a satisfactory level. Following the one-year probation, the ALJ would convert to a lifetime appointment.

REFORM FINANCIAL REGULATION AND PREVENT TAXPAYER-FUNDED BAILOUTS
Multi-Agency

As directed in the Executive Order on Core Principles for Regulating the United States Financial System issued on February 3, 2017 (Core Principles EO), the Secretary of the Treasury, with the heads of the member agencies of the Financial Stability Oversight Council, is reviewing the extent to which existing laws, regulations and other Government policies promote or inhibit these Core Principles. While exact savings will be subject to the review's outcome, the Budget includes $35 billion in anticipated savings to be realized through reforms that prevent bailouts, foster vibrant financial markets, and reverse burdensome regulations that hinder financial innovation and reduce access to credit for American families.

Funding Summary
(In millions of dollars)

	2018	2019	2020	2021	2022	2023	2024	2025	2026	2027	2018-22	2018-27
Proposed Change from Current Law..........................	0	-2,400	-3,000	-3,400	-4,300	-4,400	-4,300	-4,300	-4,400	-4,500	-13,100	-35,000

Justification

The Department of the Treasury's review will likely result in proposals that will provide significant savings to the Federal Government. Treasury's recommended legal, regulatory, and policy changes are expected to complement efforts to reverse regulatory excesses mandated by the Dodd-Frank Wall Street Reform and Consumer Protection Act (the Dodd-Frank Act). Savings resulting from Treasury's review are notionally valued at $35 billion, though the final amount is contingent upon reforms recommended in Treasury's reports to the President. Since enactment of the Dodd-Frank Act, Treasury and the Federal financial and banking regulatory Agencies have expended substantial Government resources on generating hundreds of regulations that impose a significant burden on small businesses, stifle financial innovation, and curtail Americans' access to credit.

REFORM THE MEDICAL LIABILITY SYSTEM
Multi-Agency

The Budget proposes to reform medical liability beginning in 2018. The reforms are expected to reduce healthcare costs and health insurance premiums by reducing medical liability insurance premiums and defensive medicine. Under this proposal, Federal health program costs would decrease (including in Medicare, Medicaid, Exchange subsidies, and the Federal Employee Health Benefits Program) and taxable income and payroll tax receipts would increase.

Funding Summary
(In millions of dollars)

	2018	2019	2020	2021	2022	2023	2024	2025	2026	2027	2018-22	2018-27
Proposed Change from Current Law	-179	-1,097	-1,928	-3,308	-4,827	-6,541	-8,082	-9,114	-9,642	-10,295	-11,339	-55,013

Justification

The current medical liability system does not work for patients or providers, nor does it promote high quality, evidence-based care. Providers practice with a threat of potentially frivolous lawsuits, and injured patients often do not receive just compensation for their injuries. The Budget proposes to reform medical liability and reduce defensive medicine beginning in 2018 by implementing a set of provisions to reduce the number of high dollar awards, limit liability, reduce provider burden, promote evidence-based practices, and strengthen the physician-patient relationship. Specifically, the Budget's proposals include, among others: a cap on non-economic damage awards of $250,000 (increasing with inflation over time); a three-year statute of limitations, allowing courts to modify attorney's fee arrangements, allowing evidence of a claimant's income from other sources (e.g., workers' compensation, auto insurance) to be introduced at trial, creating a safe harbor for clinicians following evidence-based clinical practice guidelines; and authorizing the Secretary to provide guidance to States to create expert panels and administrative health care tribunals to review medical liability cases. These proposals align with the Administration's priorities for reforming the health system.

REPEAL AND REPLACE OBAMACARE
Multi-Agency

The Budget includes $250 billion in deficit savings associated with health care reform as part of the President's commitment to rescue Americans from the failures of Obamacare and to expand choice, increase access, and lower premiums. The Administration applauds the House's passage of the American Health Care Act, which will remove Obamacare's burden and put in place a responsible replacement. The President is committed to working with the Congress to pass real health care reform that will benefit all Americans.

Funding Summary
(In millions of dollars)

	2018	2019	2020	2021	2022	2023	2024	2025	2026	2027	2018-22	2018-27
Proposed Change from Current Law............	25,000	30,000	-5,000	-30,000	-35,000	-40,000	-40,000	-50,000	-50,000	-55,000	-15,000	-250,000

Justification

Across the Nation, Obamacare is failing the American people, delivering high costs, few options, and broken promises. Americans across the Nation have seen their health insurance choices collapse under Obamacare, leaving an increasing number attempting to buy health insurance through the Obamacare Exchanges with only one insurer.

Without competition among insurers, Americans have been forced to buy increasingly unaffordable coverage, with premiums spiraling out of control. Obamacare premiums in some States have increased by double and triple digits. For example, premiums for Exchange plans in Arizona went up by 116 percent in 2016.

Meanwhile, American businesses have been suffering under the hundreds of billions in taxes that financed Obamacare, which are a drain on the American economy as well as ordinary families.

Obamacare is a disaster and must be repealed. Mandating every American to buy Government-approved health insurance was never the right solution for our country. Americans should have the freedom to make the decisions that are right for them and their families, and should have more choices and access to the health care they want and deserve.

The President supports a repeal and replace approach that improves Medicaid's sustainability and targets resources to those most in need, eliminates Obamacare's onerous taxes and mandates, provides funding for States to stabilize markets and ensure a smooth transition away from Obamacare, and helps Americans purchase the coverage they want through the use of tax credits and expanded Health Savings Accounts. This approach sets a foundation for a patient-centered health care system where Americans will have more choices, lower premiums, and greater access to different insurance options.

SPECTRUM AUCTIONS
Multi-Agency

The Budget proposes to extend the Federal Communications Commission's (FCC) authority to conduct auctions.

Funding Summary
(In millions of dollars)

	2018	2019	2020	2021	2022	2023	2024	2025	2026	2027	2018-22	2018-27
Proposed Change from Current Law..........................	0	0	-300	-300	0	0	0	0	0	-6,000	-600	-6,600

Justification

The Spectrum Pipeline Act of 2015 ("Act") requires the auction of 30 MHz of spectrum below 6 GHz by 2024, and extends the FCC's auction authority allowing for such auctions. Based on ongoing research authorized through the Act, the Administration anticipates that additional spectrum assignments will be made available for auction. As a result, the Budget proposes to extend the FCC's authority to conduct auctions to make any additional spectrum identified available for commercial use. Auction proceeds are expected to exceed $6 billion through 2027.

AGRICULTURAL MARKETING SERVICE USER FEE
Department of Agriculture

The Administration proposes establishing an Agricultural Marketing Service (AMS) user fee to cover the full costs of the Agency's oversight of Marketing Orders and Agreements.

Funding Summary
(In millions of dollars)

	2018	2019	2020	2021	2022	2023	2024	2025	2026	2027	2018-22	2018-27
Proposed Change from Current Law............	-20	-20	-20	-20	-20	-20	-20	-20	-20	-20	-100	-200

Justification

Marketing Orders and Agreements are initiated by industry to help provide stable markets, and are tailored to the specific industry's needs. For example, milk Marketing Orders help assure a minimum price for dairy products, while Marketing Orders and Agreements for fruits, vegetables, and other specialty crops help control supply and ensure that produce on the market maintains high-quality standards. AMS is authorized only to provide oversight of Marketing Orders and Agreements. AMS oversight responsibilities range from reviewing applications for new orders and holding hearings on proposals, to publishing Federal Register notices establishing new agreements. The industries that substantially benefit from Marketing Orders and Agreements should pay for the oversight of these programs.

ANIMAL AND PLANT HEALTH INSPECTION SERVICE USER FEE
Department of Agriculture

The Budget proposes establishing three new Animal and Plant Health Inspection Service (APHIS) user fees to offset costs related to 1) enforcement of the Animal Welfare Act; 2) regulation of biotechnology derived products; and 3) regulation of veterinary biologics products. The fees would cover costs related to licenses, registration, and authorization for regulated entities.

Funding Summary
(In millions of dollars)

	2018	2019	2020	2021	2022	2023	2024	2025	2026	2027	2018-22	2018-27
Proposed Change from Current Law	-20	-20	-20	-20	-20	-20	-20	-20	-20	-20	-100	-200

Justification

Under the authority of the Animal Welfare Act (AWA), APHIS conducts activities designed to ensure the humane care and treatment of certain animals bred for commercial sale, used in research, transported commercially or exhibited to the public. These activities include licensing, registering, and inspecting certain establishments to ensure compliance with the AWA. APHIS would charge entities for the costs associated with licensing and registration.

Under the authority of the Plant Protection Act, APHIS regulates the introduction—meaning the importation, interstate movement, and field-testing—of organisms derived through biotechnology that may pose a plant pest risk. After careful review, APHIS may issue a permit or notification to allow entities to conduct these specific activities, and conduct the necessary oversight to ensure compliance. APHIS would charge an application fee from entities seeking authorization for the introduction of biotechnology derived products.

Under the authority of the Virus-Serum-Toxin Act, APHIS regulates veterinary biologics (vaccines, bacterins, antisera, diagnostic kits, and other products of biological origin) to ensure that those products produced in or imported into the United States are not "worthless, contaminated, dangerous, or harmful." APHIS' licensing activities allow manufacturers to market their products. APHIS would charge a licensing fee to manufacturers of veterinary biologics.

ELIMINATE INTEREST PAYMENTS TO ELECTRIC AND TELECOMMUNICATIONS UTILITIES
Department of Agriculture

The Budget proposes to eliminate the interest accrual on future deposits in the Rural Utilities Service borrowers' *cushion of credit* accounts. The program is unnecessary since rural electric and telecommunications cooperatives can find comparable investment options in the private sector.

Funding Summary
(In millions of dollars)

	2018	2019	2020	2021	2022	2023	2024	2025	2026	2027	2018-22	2018-27
Proposed Change from Current Law............	-131	-136	-136	-140	-142	-137	-138	-139	-139	-139	-685	-1,377

Justification

The *cushion of credit* program was authorized in 1987 as part of an omnibus reconciliation package. It set up a program to encourage rural electric and telecommunications borrowers to repay their Rural Utilities Service (RUS) debt. Under the program, borrowers make voluntary deposits into *cushion of credit* accounts and use those deposits to make their scheduled payments on loans made or guaranteed by RUS. The borrower earns interest on these deposits at a rate of five percent. Rural electric and telecommunications utility borrowers do not need these unique interest payments to guarantee loan repayment, especially when the private sector offers comparable investment options.

ELIMINATE THE RURAL ECONOMIC DEVELOPMENT PROGRAM
Department of Agriculture

The Budget proposes to eliminate the interest accrual on future deposits in the Rural Utilities Service borrowers' *cushion of credit* accounts, including the interest that is paid to the Rural Economic Development Grant account to pay for rural economic grants and loans. This change is consistent with other Budget proposals that eliminate rural business programs.

Funding Summary
(In millions of dollars)

	2018	2019	2020	2021	2022	2023	2024	2025	2026	2027	2018-22	2018-27
Proposed Change from Current Law	-6	-154	-158	-159	0	0	0	0	0	0	-477	-477

Justification

Year after year, the Government Accountability Office includes the Rural Business & Cooperative Service (RBS) in its annual report on fragmentation, overlap, and duplication, and the Department of Agriculture's (USDA) Inspector General found two of the Agency's largest loan and grant programs to be improperly managed. RBS programs lack program evaluation, so it has not been possible to assess program impact. USDA has not been able to demonstrate that these programs meet the broader goals of reducing rural poverty, out-migration, or unemployment.

The Administration's tax, regulatory, and infrastructure policies are expected to be more effective at improving rural economies and job growth.

FARM BILL SAVINGS
Department of Agriculture

The Budget proposes to use means testing to target assistance to those that need it most, and to eliminate programs that have not demonstrated outcomes or are not a Federal responsibility. Specifically, the Budget proposes to: target commodity assistance, crop insurance subsidies, and conservation assistance to producers that have an Adjusted Gross Income (AGI) of $500,000 or less; limit each farmer or entity to $40,000 in crop insurance premium subsidies; eliminate the ability for producers to purchase subsidized insurance that insures their crops at the higher of the price projected at planting, or that at harvest; eliminate funding for a number of programs for which there is no Federal purpose; and better target conservation funding to the most sensitive agricultural land.

Funding Summary
(In millions of dollars)

	2018	2019	2020	2021	2022	2023	2024	2025	2026	2027	2018-22	2018-27
$40K Crop Insurance Premium Subsidy Limit	0	-1,552	-1,620	-1,815	-1,826	-1,845	-1,856	-1,885	-1,897	-1,920	-6,813	-16,216
$500K AGI Eligibility Limit	-72	-94	-112	-113	-113	-112	-113	-113	-114	-117	-504	-1,073
Eliminate Harvest Price Option for Crop Insurance	0	-1,212	-1,251	-1,314	-1,325	-1,335	-1,353	-1,365	-1,378	-1,390	-5,102	-11,923
Streamline Conservation	-84	-210	-272	-319	-402	-560	-716	-886	-1,072	-1,234	-1,287	-5,755
Eliminate Small Programs	-111	-304	-313	-339	-335	-335	-335	-335	-335	-335	-1,402	-3,077
Total	-267	-3,372	-3,568	-3,900	-4,001	-4,188	-4,373	-4,584	-4,797	-4,996	-15,108	-38,046

Justification

The Budget proposes to eliminate premium subsidies and commodity payments for farmers with Adjusted Gross Incomes over $500,000. It is hard to justify to hardworking taxpayers why the Federal Government should provide assistance to wealthy farmers with incomes over a half million dollars. Doing so undermines the credibility and purpose of farm programs. In 2013 (a year of record-high farm income), only 2.1 percent of farmers had Adjusted Gross Incomes over $500,000.

The Budget proposes to limit farmers to $40,000 in premium subsidies. Setting a limit on premium subsidies for crop insurance is consistent with how commodity payments are treated, and will reduce the generous Federal subsidies that this program has been providing. In 2011, 26 farm businesses benefitted from $1 million in premium subsidies, and more than 10,000 received more than $100,000 in premium subsidies. According to a 2012 Government Accountability Office (GAO) study, had such a limit been applied in 2011, it would have affected up to 3.9 percent of all participating farmers, who accounted for about one-third of all premium subsidies and were primarily associated with large farms.

The subsidy the Government currently provides farmers averages 62 percent of their crop insurance premiums, with no limit to the amount of subsidy any farmer can receive. It is no longer necessary to provide unlimited subsidies for crop insurance premium payments. The majority of farmers participating in crop insurance are also eligible for commodity payments. The Department of Agriculture tracks participation for the top 10 crops they insure, nine of which receive other commodity payments.

Furthermore, the Budget proposes to no longer allow farmers to insure their crops at the *higher* of the price at planting and that at harvest. Producers that want to hedge their risk can purchase unsubsidized harvest price coverage, or use futures and options on mercantile exchanges, as they did before subsidized Harvest Price Option was offered.

The Budget also proposes to streamline conservation program funding by increasing funding to those programs that have shown positive outcomes and eliminating funding to those that have not.

Further, the Budget proposes to eliminate programs for which there is no Federal purpose. The Government should not be subsidizing the advertising and promotion of commodities, singling out select commodities for special assistance, or providing subsidies to producers for the processing of their products.

FOOD SAFETY AND INSPECTION SERVICE USER FEE
Department of Agriculture

The Budget proposes establishing a Food Safety and Inspection Service (FSIS) user fee to cover the costs of all domestic inspection activity, import re-inspection, and most of the central operations costs for Federal, State, and International inspection programs for meat, poultry, and eggs.

Funding Summary
(In millions of dollars)

	2018	2019	2020	2021	2022	2023	2024	2025	2026	2027	2018-22	2018-27
Proposed Change from Current Law..........	0	-660	-660	-660	-660	-660	-660	-660	-660	-660	-2,640	-5,940

Justification

FSIS inspections benefit the meat, poultry, and egg industries. FSIS personnel are continuously present for all egg processing and domestic slaughter operations, inspect each livestock and poultry carcass, and inspect operations at meat and poultry processing establishments at least once per shift. The inspections cover microbiological and chemical testing, as well as cleanliness and cosmetic product defects. The "inspected by USDA" stamp on meat and poultry labels increases consumer confidence in the product which may increase sales. The proposed user fee would not cover Federal functions such as investigation, enforcement, risk analysis, and emergency response. The Administration estimates this fee would increase the cost of meat, poultry, and eggs for consumers by less than one cent per pound.

GRAIN INSPECTION, PACKERS AND STOCKYARDS ADMINISTRATION USER FEE
Department of Agriculture

The Budget proposes establishing two Grain Inspection, Packers and Stockyards Administration (GIPSA) user fees, to recover costs for 1) the development, review, and maintenance of official U.S. grain standards; and 2) licensing of livestock market agencies, dealers, stockyards, packers, and swine contractors.

Funding Summary
(In millions of dollars)

	2018	2019	2020	2021	2022	2023	2024	2025	2026	2027	2018-22	2018-27
Proposed Change from Current Law...............	-30	-30	-30	-30	-30	-30	-30	-30	-30	-30	-150	-300

Justification

The first proposed fee would be administered by GIPSA's Federal Grain Inspection Service, which develops and maintains quality U.S. grain standards to facilitate the grain trade. The entities that directly benefit from these standards would pay for the costs of standardization. Currently, entities pay a fee for the service they receive for the inspection and weighing of grain, and this proposal extends the fee to standardization. The second proposed fee would cover costs for GIPSA's Packers and Stockyards Program, which benefits the livestock, meat, and poultry industries by promoting fair business practices and competitive market environments.

SNAP REFORMS
Department of Agriculture

The Budget proposes a suite of legislative proposals aimed at targeting Supplemental Nutrition Assistance Program (SNAP) benefits to the neediest households, and encouraging work among able-bodied adults without dependents. The Budget also proposes to re-balance the Federal/State partnership in SNAP benefits to low-income households by gradually establishing a State match for benefit costs, phasing in from a national average of 10 percent in 2020 to 25 percent, on average by 2023. Combined, these reforms would generate nearly $191 billion in savings over 10 years.

Funding Summary
(In millions of dollars)

	2018	2019	2020	2021	2022	2023	2024	2025	2026	2027	2018-22	2018-27
Proposed Change from Current Law...............	-4,637	-7,627	-13,990	-16,928	-21,130	-24,871	-24,634	-25,714	-26,135	-25,266	-64,312	-190,932

Justification

SNAP provides low-income households with electronic benefits they can use to buy groceries at authorized retailers. As a primary component of the social safety net, SNAP has grown significantly in the past decade. As expected, SNAP participation grew to historic levels during the recession. However, despite improvements in unemployment since the recession ended, SNAP participation remains persistently high.

The Budget proposes a series of reforms aimed at right-sizing SNAP's share of the Budget. Reforms include closing eligibility loopholes by limiting categorical eligibility to participants receiving cash benefits from TANF or SSI; modifying income and benefit calculations to ensure benefits are targeted to the neediest households; and limiting the use of waivers that exempt able-bodied adults without dependents from the expectation that they work.

Under the State match proposal, States would cover a portion of the cost of benefits issued to participants. A State's share of the cost would be based on a formula that incorporates the economic indicators that drive SNAP participation along with State resources. The Budget assumes the match would be phased in gradually, beginning with a national average of 10 percent in 2020 and increasing to an average rate of 25 percent by 2023. To help States manage their costs, new flexibility regarding benefit levels would be provided. This proposal also assumes that, in cases of natural disaster, D-SNAP benefits would continue to be 100 percent federally funded.

This proposal allows States to determine their level of SNAP benefits. It is fairly and reasonably designed and gives States options that can mitigate the effects of the funding shift. By giving States a financial stake in the cost of providing these benefits, rather than relying entirely on Federal funds, it would increase State incentives to create economic paths to self-sufficiency.

SNAP RETAILER APPLICATION FEE
Department of Agriculture

The Budget proposes establishment of an application fee for retailers seeking authorization to accept and redeem the electronic benefits provided by the Supplemental Nutrition Assistance Program (SNAP), formerly Food Stamps. Currently, retailers do not pay a fee to become authorized, which fails to recognize the Federal costs of application processing and oversight of retailers, and the significant portion of a retailer's revenue that SNAP can represent. This proposal is estimated to generate approximately $2.4 billion in revenue over 10 years to offset SNAP expenses.

Funding Summary
(In millions of dollars)

	2018	2019	2020	2021	2022	2023	2024	2025	2026	2027	2018-22	2018-27
Proposed Change from Current Law..........................	-252	-246	-241	-236	-230	-230	-230	-230	-230	-230	-1,205	-2,355

Justification

The Department of Agriculture authorizes and oversees participation by retail food outlets participating in SNAP. Interested retailers must meet eligibility criteria, apply and be authorized before accepting SNAP benefits, and periodically reauthorize in order to continue participation. In 2016, over $66 billion in SNAP benefits were redeemed by about 260,000 authorized retailers in the United States.

Under this proposal, an authorization/reauthorization fee would be scaled upon existing retailer size and category definitions, ranging from $250 for the smallest firms, such as small convenience stores, to as much as $20,000 for the largest retailers, such as super-centers and large supermarket chains. Retailers would pay the fee each time they are authorized or reauthorized.

CREATE SINGLE INCOME-DRIVEN REPAYMENT PLAN
Department of Education

The Budget proposes to simplify student loan repayment by consolidating multiple Income-Driven Repayment (IDR) plans into a single plan. This proposal reduces inefficiencies in the student loan program by establishing several reforms to guarantee that all borrowers in IDR pay an equitable share of their income, and for undergraduate borrowers, reduce the time until loans are forgiven.

Funding Summary
(In millions of dollars)

	2018	2019	2020	2021	2022	2023	2024	2025	2026	2027	2018-22	2018-27
Single IDR Plan	-1,685	-3,333	-5,317	-6,830	-8,141	-9,060	-9,972	-10,394	-10,726	-10,946	-25,306	-76,404

Justification

In recent years, IDR plans, which offer student borrowers the option of making affordable monthly payments based on factors such as income and family size, have grown in popularity. However, the numerous IDR plans currently offered to borrowers overly complicate choosing and enrolling in the right plan. To simplify student loan repayment, the Budget proposes a single IDR plan that provides a pathway to debt relief for struggling borrowers. All new borrowers would pay 12.5 percent of their discretionary income. For borrowers with undergraduate student debt only, any balance remaining after 15 years of repayment would be forgiven. For borrowers with any graduate debt, any balance remaining after 30 years of repayment would be forgiven. To support this ambitious proposal, the Budget proposes a package of targeted reforms to reduce significant inefficiencies in the program. The single IDR plan would remove the standard repayment cap to guarantee that high-income, high-balance borrowers pay an equitable share before their remaining balances are forgiven. In addition, the proposed plan would calculate payments for married borrowers filing separately using their combined household Adjusted Gross Income.

ELIMINATE ACCOUNT MAINTENANCE FEE PAYMENTS TO GUARANTY AGENCIES
Department of Education

The Budget proposes to eliminate unnecessary fee payments to guaranty agencies.

Funding Summary
(In millions of dollars)

	2018	2019	2020	2021	2022	2023	2024	2025	2026	2027	2018-22	2018-27
Eliminate AMFs	-443	0	0	0	0	0	0	0	0	0	-443	-443

Justification

Despite dwindling business activities since the move to direct student lending, guaranty agencies from the legacy Federal Family Education Loan (FFEL) Program continue to get paid account maintenance fees. Given the significantly pared back services provided by guaranty agencies, and their ability to generate significant fee income through debt collection activities, the Budget proposes to discontinue these payments.

ELIMINATE PUBLIC SERVICE LOAN FORGIVENESS
Department of Education

The Budget proposes to eliminate the Public Service Loan Forgiveness (PSLF) program and focus assistance on needy undergraduate student borrowers from all professions.

Funding Summary
(In millions of dollars)

	2018	2019	2020	2021	2022	2023	2024	2025	2026	2027	2018-22	2018-27
Eliminate PSLF	-859	-1,466	-2,179	-2,679	-3,030	-3,263	-3,493	-3,575	-3,491	-3,436	-10,213	-27,471

Justification

To support the proposal for a single Income-Driven Repayment (IDR) plan, the Budget proposes a package of targeted student loan reforms and program eliminations, including the elimination of PSLF. PSLF unfairly favors some career choices over others and is complicated for borrowers to navigate. This package would simplify repayment for all new undergraduate borrowers regardless of occupation and create a pathway for expedited debt forgiveness after 15 years of payments instead of after 20 years under current law. PSLF is part of a complex array of Federal aid programs that could benefit from the simplification of aid to needy students. The Budget would help low-income students afford college through Pell Grants, now expanded to fund Year-round Pell Grants that would enable students to complete their degrees faster.

ELIMINATE SUBSIDIZED LOANS
Department of Education

The Budget proposes to eliminate inefficient interest subsidies for certain undergraduate loans and focus resources on more effective forms of support for needy undergraduate students.

Funding Summary
(In millions of dollars)

	2018	2019	2020	2021	2022	2023	2024	2025	2026	2027	2018-22	2018-27
Eliminate Subsidized Loans..................	-1,052	-2,157	-3,098	-3,791	-4,199	-4,499	-4,744	-4,960	-5,145	-5,228	-14,297	-38,873

Justification

To support the proposal for a single Income-Driven Repayment (IDR) plan, the Budget proposes a package of targeted reforms and program eliminations, including the elimination of subsidized loans. While the in-school interest subsidy has not been rigorously evaluated, lessons from behavioral economics indicate that the subsidy is less likely to increase postsecondary enrollment, due to the complexity of the interest rate benefit, than straightforward need-based grants to students. The subsidy is also poorly targeted as it is provided to borrowers with low pre-enrollment income but does not consider the income of borrowers during repayment. Borrowers with unaffordable debt burdens relative to their income during repayment can manage their debt through income-driven repayment and ultimately receive forgiveness. Subsidized loans are part of a complex array of Federal aid programs that could benefit from the simplification of aid to needy students. The Budget would help low-income students afford college through Pell Grants, which would be expanded to fund Year-round Pell Grants that would enable students to complete their degrees faster.

POWER MARKETING ADMINISTRATION TRANSMISSION ASSET DIVESTITURE
Department of Energy

Funding Summary
(In millions of dollars)

	2018	2019	2020	2021	2022	2023	2024	2025	2026	2027	2018-22	2018-27
Divest SWPA Transmission Assets.........	0	-13	0	0	0	0	0	0	0	0	-13	-13
Divest WAPA Transmission Assets.........	0	-580	0	0	0	0	0	0	0	0	-580	-580
Divest BPA Transmission Assets.........	0	-1,821	-396	-386	-386	-386	-386	-386	-386	-386	-2,989	-4,919
Total.........	0	-2,414	-396	-386	-386	-386	-386	-386	-386	-386	-3,582	-5,512

The Budget proposes to divest the transmission assets of the Power Marketing Administrations (PMAs), which include Southwestern Power Administration (SWPA), Western Area Power Administration (WAPA), and Bonneville Power Administration (BPA).

Justification

The vast majority of the Nation's electricity infrastructure is owned and operated by for-profit investor owned utilities. Ownership of transmission assets is best carried out by the private sector where there are appropriate market and regulatory incentives. The Budget proposal to eliminate or reduce the PMA's role in electricity transmission and increase the private sector's role would encourage a more efficient allocation of economic resources and mitigate risk to taxpayers.

REPEAL BORROWING AUTHORITY FOR WESTERN AREA POWER ADMINISTRATION
Department of Energy

The Budget proposes to repeal Western Area Power Administration's (WAPA) authority to borrow up to $3.25 billion in emergency funds authorized by the American Recovery and Reinvestment Act of 2009 (Recovery Act) for the purpose of constructing and/or funding projects within WAPA's service territory that deliver, or facilitate the delivery of, power generated by renewable energy resources.

Funding Summary
(In millions of dollars)

	2018	2019	2020	2021	2022	2023	2024	2025	2026	2027	2018-22	2018-27
Proposed Change from Current Law...............	-610	-900	-1,095	-660	-725	-235	-50	-50	-50	-50	-3,990	-4,425

Justification

The vast majority of the Nation's electricity needs are met through for-profit investor-owned utilities. Investments in transmission assets are best carried out by the private sector where there are appropriate market and regulatory incentives. Federal financing of transmission assets places unnecessary risk on taxpayers and results in an inefficient allocation of economic resources. Further, activities under the Recovery Act, which was enacted in response to the Great Recession, are no longer needed. Since its inception, the program has made less than $300 million in total loans to three transmission projects. As of fiscal year-end 2016, the program held less than $100 million in outstanding loan balances owed to Treasury.

STRATEGIC PETROLEUM RESERVE - REDUCE BY HALF
Department of Energy

The Budget proposes statutory changes that would allow the Department of Energy (DOE) to sell approximately 270 million barrels of Strategic Petroleum Reserve (SPR) crude oil, roughly half of what remains after current law sales, as well as reduce modernization funding by half ($1 billion), and close two of the four SPR sites, all by 2027. A path to energy security means enabling more American production and investment, not having the Government store an unnecessarily large amount of oil underground.

Funding Summary
(In millions of dollars)

	2018	2019	2020	2021	2022	2023	2024	2025	2026	2027	2018-22	2018-27
Proposed Change from Current Law	-500	-500	-552	-1,390	-1,426	-1,489	-1,519	-1,549	-3,793	-3,868	-4,368	-16,586

Justification

Enabling domestic fossil energy production and investment is a key component of increasing U.S. energy security, and today the United States is producing oil and gas like never before. In 2016, the United States produced nearly 8.9 million barrels of crude oil per day, and over 26.4 trillion cubic feet of natural gas-up from 5.6 million barrels per day (+59 percent) and 22.9 trillion cubic feet (+15 percent) in 2011. Moreover, tomorrow's energy security will be enhanced by eliminating burdensome Federal regulations and red tape to better enable new, private investment and harness the United States' full energy potential. The SPR is a product of the 1970s, an era when the United States imported 5-6 million barrels of oil per day from the Organization of Petroleum Exporting Countries (OPEC), compared to now where imports from OPEC countries are roughly half that amount, despite a significantly larger economy. The independent Energy Information Administration (EIA) at DOE now projects our net petroleum product imports to decline to less than 2 million barrels per day by 2027, down from roughly 5 million barrels per day in 2016.[1] Thus, the proposal to reduce the SPR to about half of its future (2027) size, with or without additional private stocks, would very likely provide sufficient protection in the event of an energy crisis and would maintain compliance with international agreements.

Citations

[1] Department of Energy, Energy Information Administration: *Annual Energy Outlook 2017*, (January 2017).

ELIMINATE THE SOCIAL SERVICES BLOCK GRANT
Department of Health and Human Services

The Budget proposes to eliminate the Social Services Block Grant (SSBG) because it lacks strong performance measures, is not well targeted, and is not a core function of the Federal Government. States do not have to demonstrate that they are using funds effectively in order to continue receiving funding. In addition, SSBG funds services that are also funded through other Federal programs, such as early childhood education services funded through Head Start and child welfare services funded by Title IV-E programs.

Funding Summary
(In millions of dollars)

	2018	2019	2020	2021	2022	2023	2024	2025	2026	2027	2018-22	2018-27
Proposed Change from Current Law..........................	-1,393	-1,661	-1,677	-1,677	-1,677	-1,677	-1,677	-1,677	-1,677	-1,677	-8,085	-16,470

Justification

SSBG is a permanently authorized program, which funds a wide variety of services. There are 29 broad service categories within SSBG (including "other"). However, better targeted State and Federal programs currently fund most of these services. SSBG lacks strong performance metrics and the means to hold States accountable for spending SSBG funds effectively.

REFORM MEDICAID
Department of Health and Human Services

To realign financial incentives and provide stability to both Federal and State budgets, the Budget proposes to reform Medicaid by giving States the choice between a per capita cap and a block grant starting in 2020, which would empower States to innovate and refocus their Medicaid programs on the most vulnerable populations. In addition, the Budget would provide States with more flexibility to control costs and design individual, State-based solutions to provide better care to Medicaid beneficiaries.

Funding Summary
(In millions of dollars)

	2018	2019	2020	2021	2022	2023	2024	2025	2026	2027	2018-22	2018-27
Proposed Change from Current Law..........	0	0	-10,000	-20,000	-40,000	-60,000	-80,000	-105,000	-130,000	-165,000	-70,000	-610,000

Justification

Current growth in Medicaid spending is unsustainable, with growth outpacing gross domestic product and national health spending and accounting for an increasing share of Federal and State budgets. The current open-ended structure of Federal Medicaid funding encourages States to shift costs to the Federal Government and does not encourage States to focus on preventing waste, fraud, and abuse. At the State level, Medicaid crowds out important State priorities such as investments in education, public safety, and infrastructure. Medicaid's outdated rules are restrictive and complex, tying States' hands and preventing States from designing innovative approaches that address the specific needs of their populations.

The Budget would reverse this trend by simplifying the financing structure of Medicaid, and slowing future growth in Medicaid spending. Under this proposal, starting in 2020, States would have the choice of either a per capita cap or a block grant, and will receive new flexibility to design and operate their programs, such as encouraging work and personal responsibility. The proposal to reform Federal Medicaid funding and provide new flexibility to States, would allow States to refocus their programs on those who are most vulnerable and to develop State-specific innovations while lowering costs. The Budget would help set Medicaid on a sustainable path and ensure the program could continue to provide care to those who are most vulnerable, the elderly, individuals with disabilities, children, and pregnant women.

STRENGTHEN THE CHILD SUPPORT ENFORCEMENT PROGRAM
Department of Health and Human Services

The Budget includes a number of proposals that strengthen the Child Support Enforcement Program, which would provide State Agencies additional tools to increase efficiency, facilitate family self-sufficiency, and promote responsible parenthood.

Funding Summary
(In millions of dollars)

	2018	2019	2020	2021	2022	2023	2024	2025	2026	2027	2018-22	2018-27
Strengthening Child Support Enforcement and Establishment Package.........	-22	-35	-54	-68	-85	-86	-87	-90	-90	-91	-264	-708
Establish a Child Support Technology Fund...................	-110	-122	-120	-121	-136	-43	-48	-55	-36	-42	-609	-833

Justification

The package of Child Support Establishment and Enforcement proposals in the Budget would increase child support collections, which would result in savings to Federal benefits programs. For example, by requiring additional data matches and reporting throughout child support establishment and enforcement processes, the proposal would expand and improve the ability to intercept sources of income for payment of child support, including insurance settlements, lump-sum payments provided by employers, gaming winnings from casinos, and State workers' compensation claims. The package would also improve enforcement procedures related to freezing and seizing certain assets held by delinquent non-custodial parents, and would require the reporting of independent contractors to State directories used to locate non-custodial parents and identify sources of income. The proposal would also provide States with access to better financial data matching programs, as well as tools that promote interstate cooperation.

In addition, the proposal to create a Child Support Technology Fund would facilitate the replacement of aging IT systems in State child support programs, and increase security, efficiency, and program integrity. This proposal would provide States the option to acquire a model child support system and various applications. This approach would reduce inefficiencies associated with the current process of modernizing child support IT systems, which involves each State separately designing, developing, and implementing a new system, with costs ranging between $80 and $120 million per State. The Federal Government shares these costs through 66 percent Federal reimbursement. With States using The Department of Health and Human Services (HHS)-developed technology made possible by the Fund, the Federal Government would avoid reimbursing up to 54 times over the costs associated with building new State systems. Leveraging reusable technology would provide a cost effective solution to the widespread and pressing issue of replacing aging State child support systems.

TEMPORARY ASSISTANCE FOR NEEDY FAMILIES REFORMS
Department of Health and Human Services

The Budget proposes to reduce the portion of the Temporary Assistance for Needy Families (TANF) block grant (10 percent) that States may transfer from TANF to Social Services Block Grant (SSBG). The Budget also proposes to eliminate the TANF Contingency Fund, as it fails to provide well-targeted counter-cyclical funding to States.

Funding Summary
(In millions of dollars)

	2018	2019	2020	2021	2022	2023	2024	2025	2026	2027	2018-22	2018-27
Reduce TANF Block Grant by 10%...	-1,218	-1,491	-1,550	-1,582	-1,615	-1,632	-1,632	-1,632	-1,632	-1,632	-7,456	-15,616
Eliminate the TANF Contingency Fund...	-567	-608	-608	-608	-608	-608	-608	-608	-608	-608	-2,999	-6,039
Total...	-1,785	-2,099	-2,158	-2,190	-2,223	-2,240	-2,240	-2,240	-2,240	-2,240	-10,455	-21,655

Justification

The Budget would reduce the TANF block grant by 10 percent, which aligns with the Budget proposal to eliminate the SSBG. While the proposal would reduce the amount available to States for cash assistance and other benefits that promote self-sufficiency, the proposal also recognizes that TANF's flexible spending rules have resulted in States using a large portion of TANF funds for benefits and services that do not directly serve the core intent of the program – to help low-income families meet their basic needs and move them towards self-sufficiency. Under the proposal, States would continue to have broad flexibility in determining how to spend their remaining TANF block grant funds, and could choose to focus a greater share on welfare-to-work activities.

The Budget also proposes to eliminate the TANF Contingency Fund, recognizing its failure to provide well-targeted counter-cyclical funding to States. While the intent of the Contingency Fund has been to assist States experiencing increased demand for cash assistance during economic downturns, States may use contingency funds for any TANF purpose, many of which have no direct relationship to helping families meet needs in hard economic times. Some States have used contingency funds to simply replace existing block grant funds (i.e., building up their unobligated balances), without actually spending more to address increased need. In addition, because the triggers for eligibility for the Contingency Fund have not been updated, all States except Wyoming have been eligible for the Fund in every month since June 2009. The States that have accessed the Fund are not necessarily those that need it most, but rather those that could identify the necessary amount of State spending needed to meet the higher maintenance-of-effort requirement associated with receipt of contingency funds.

EXTEND EXPIRING CUSTOMS AND BORDER PROTECTION FEES
Department of Homeland Security

This proposal would re-authorize Customs User Fees set to expire on September 30, 2025.

Funding Summary
(In millions of dollars)

	2018	2019	2020	2021	2022	2023	2024	2025	2026	2027	2018-22	2018-27
Proposed Change from Current Law..........................	0	0	0	0	0	0	0	0	-3,931	-4,143	0	-8,074

Justification

The authorization to collect and spend several U.S. Customs and Border Protection user fees authorized in 9 U.S.C. 58c expires on September 30, 2025. This proposal would extend the authorization to collect and spend these fees through the end of the Budget window.

REFORM OF THE NATIONAL FLOOD INSURANCE PROGRAM
Department of Homeland Security

The Budget includes a National Flood Insurance Program (NFIP) reform proposal that would put the program on a more sustainable financial footing moving forward, expand flood insurance coverage by encouraging private competition in the flood insurance market, and incentivize mitigation measures by signaling to homeowners the true cost associated with the risk of living in a floodplain. The estimated savings from doing so are almost $8.9 billion over 10 years.

Funding Summary
(In millions of dollars)

	2018	2019	2020	2021	2022	2023	2024	2025	2026	2027	2018-22	2018-27
Proposed Change from Current Law..........	-95	-301	-509	-730	-971	-1,076	-1,141	-1,260	-1,375	-1,432	-2,606	-8,890

Justification

The Federal Government provides flood insurance through the NFIP, which is administered by the Federal Emergency Management Agency (FEMA). Flood insurance is available to homeowners and businesses in communities that have adopted and enforce appropriate floodplain management measures. At the end of 2016, the program had an estimated 5.1 million policies in more than 22,200 communities with approximately $1.25 trillion of insurance in force.

NFIP has operated at a loss since Hurricane Katrina struck the Gulf Coast in 2005. Past catastrophic flood events have driven the program into debt, and the program currently owes the U.S. Treasury $24.6 billion. The catastrophic nature of flooding masks structural factors responsible for the NFIP's financial situation: the program cannot cover its costs, let alone catastrophic flood events, because of statutorily-mandated subsidies and discounts for certain classes of policyholders. Not only is the NFIP unlikely to repay its debt, but the projected interest payments for carrying this debt are also beyond its foreseeable financial capacity.

The Budget would seek to close the NFIP's budgetary shortfall and begin to decrease the NFIP's debt. The estimates reflect the Administration's desire to work with the Congress to make the program fiscally sustainable over time, and begin paying down the NFIP's debt. If fully enacted, the proposal would result in savings of approximately $8.9 billion from 2018 through 2027.

These measures would also yield non-financial benefits. The Budget would expand flood insurance coverage in the United States by leveling the playing field for the private sector to provide flood insurance coverage to consumers. By demonstrating to homeowners the true cost of living in a flood plain, the proposal would also incentivize mitigation of flood risk before disasters occur, thereby avoiding the pain and hardship of losing a home to flooding.

CANCEL SOUTHERN NEVADA PUBLIC LANDS MANAGEMENT ACT BALANCES
Department of the Interior

This proposal cancels $230 million in unobligated balances in a special account established under the Southern Nevada Public Lands Management Act (SNPLMA), which has already generated over $3 billion in projects for Nevada. This proposal would only reduce a portion of the over $600 million in remaining balances and would not affect amounts currently allocated under the law for specific uses, such as projects in the Lake Tahoe area.

Funding Summary
(In millions of dollars)

	2018	2019	2020	2021	2022	2023	2024	2025	2026	2027	2018-22	2018-27
Proposed Change from Current Law.............	-83	-69	-78	0	0	0	0	0	0	0	-230	-230

Justification

Enacted in 1998, SNPLMA authorizes the Bureau of Land Management (BLM) to sell specified public lands around Las Vegas, NV, and retain 85 percent of the proceeds in a special account to use for capital improvements and various conservation, restoration, and recreational purposes at the Interior Secretary's discretion. Since its enactment, the Department of the Interior has received over $3.4 billion from land sales under SNPLMA authority, and the proceeds have funded over 1,200 projects, with notable investments across Southern Nevada and in Lakes Tahoe and Mead.

FEDERAL LAND TRANSACTION ACT REAUTHORIZATION
Department of the Interior

This proposal would restore the Federal Land Transaction Facilitation Act (FLTFA), which expired in 2011. FLTFA facilitates the disposal of surplus lands, as identified in the Department of the Interior's Bureau of Land Management (BLM) and the Department of Agriculture's Forest Service (USFS) management plans, by allowing BLM and USFS to use the receipts to acquire 'high conservation value' lands.

Funding Summary
(In millions of dollars)

	2018	2019	2020	2021	2022	2023	2024	2025	2026	2027	2018-22	2018-27
Proposed Change from Current Law..........................	-5	-6	-9	-12	-3	0	0	0	0	0	-35	-35

Justification

The proposal would reauthorize FLTFA to allow BLM and USFS to retain receipts from the sale of lands identified as suitable for disposal in recent land use plans. Receipts would be used to fund the acquisition of environmentally sensitive lands and cover the administrative costs associated with conducting sales. First enacted in 2000, FLTFA was effective in encouraging BLM and USFS to pursue the sale or exchange of public lands identified for disposal under land use plans. At the same time, it provided an alternative source of funding to support the acquisition of sensitive lands, such as inholdings within or parcels adjacent to certain federally designated areas that contain exceptional resources. Before the authorization expired in 2011, FLTFA required that 80 percent of the receipts be spent in the same State in which the funds were generated, with the remaining funds available for acquisition in any of the 11 other Western States. The current proposal would continue this requirement.

GULF OF MEXICO ENERGY SECURITY ACT REPEAL
Department of the Interior

The Budget proposes to redirect, to Federal taxpayers, revenue sharing payments set to be paid to select Gulf Coast States from oil and gas development in Federal offshore waters. These payments, as allocated under the Gulf of Mexico Energy Security Act of 2006 (GOMESA), benefit only a small handful of States, and not all U.S. taxpayers despite Federal waters belonging to all Americans.

Funding Summary
(In millions of dollars)

	2018	2019	2020	2021	2022	2023	2024	2025	2026	2027	2018-22	2018-27
Proposed Change from Current Law..........................	-272	-327	-344	-366	-376	-375	-375	-375	-375	-375	-1,685	-3,560

Justification

Enacted in 2006, GOMESA established permanent new revenue sharing requirements for Federal Outer Continental Shelf (OCS) oil and gas revenues, and is exclusive to the Gulf Coast States of Texas, Louisiana, Alabama, and Mississippi. GOMESA deferred most payments until 2018, so the States have yet to begin receiving these funds. Under GOMESA, these States and their local jurisdictions receive 37.5 percent of OCS revenues generated from certain OCS leases. Another 12.5 percent of these revenues are allocated to permanent mandatory spending for Land and Water Conservation Fund (LWCF) grants to all States. However, Federal waters belong to all Americans, so the returns from development should come back to all taxpayers. Gulf Coast States currently receive significant economic benefits from activity in their States associated with offshore energy development.

LEASE OIL AND GAS IN ARCTIC NATIONAL WILDLIFE REFUGE
Department of the Interior

The Budget proposes legislation to authorize oil and gas leasing in a small part of the Arctic National Wildlife Refuge (ANWR), as a component of the Administration's energy development strategy. Revenues would initially be derived from bonus bids during the lease sales, with additional receipts collected once production begins.

Funding Summary
(In millions of dollars)

	2018	2019	2020	2021	2022	2023	2024	2025	2026	2027	2018-22	2018-27
Proposed Change from Current Law..........................	0	0	0	0	-400	-500	0	0	-400	-500	-400	-1,800

Justification

The Budget assumes legislation to authorize leasing for oil and gas in the coastal plain (the "1002 area") of ANWR. The first lease sale would begin around 2022/2023, allowing adequate time for the completion of appropriate environmental reviews and an updated assessment of the state of the oil and gas markets and lease bidding potential prior to scheduling specific lease sales. Additional lease sale(s) would be held in 2026/2027. Revenues would be shared equally with the State of Alaska, with most of the savings over the next 10 years derived from bonus bids paid during the lease sales. Additional revenues would be generated in the future from royalties.

The environmentally responsible development of a small portion of ANWR would be part of a broader effort to reduce the Nation's dependence on foreign energy sources. Production will take time, so it is imperative to authorize ANWR leasing now.

REPEAL ENHANCED GEOTHERMAL PAYMENTS TO COUNTIES
Department of the Interior

The Budget proposes to repeal Section 224(b) of the Energy Policy Act of 2005 to permanently discontinue payments to counties and restore the disposition of Federal geothermal leasing revenues to the historical formula of 50 percent to the States and 50 percent to the Treasury.

Funding Summary
(In millions of dollars)

	2018	2019	2020	2021	2022	2023	2024	2025	2026	2027	2018-22	2018-27
Proposed Change from Current Law............	-3	-3	-3	-4	-4	-4	-4	-4	-4	-4	-17	-37

Justification

The Energy Policy Act of 2005 changed the distribution of receipts from geothermal leases to provide 50 percent to States, 25 percent to counties, and 25 to the Federal Government. In almost all other situations where leasing revenues are generated on Federal lands, the receipts are split between the Federal Government and the affected State. The extra 25 percent in county payments are inconsistent with this longstanding revenue-sharing approach, and effectively reduce the return to Federal taxpayers from geothermal leases on Federal lands.

PENSION BENEFIT GUARANTY CORPORATION MULTIEMPLOYER PREMIUMS
Department of Labor

The Budget proposes to improve the solvency of the Pension Benefit Guaranty Corporation (PBGC) by increasing the insurance premiums paid by underfunded multiemployer pension plans. PBGC premiums are currently far lower than what a private financial institution would charge for insuring the same risk. The proposed premium reforms would improve PBGC's financial condition and are expected to be sufficient to fund the multiemployer program for the next 20 years.

Funding Summary
(In millions of dollars)

	2018	2019	2020	2021	2022	2023	2024	2025	2026	2027	2018-22	2018-27
PBGC Multiemployer Premiums	-1,196	-1,202	-1,210	-1,294	-1,507	-1,625	-1,705	-1,546	-2,238	-2,335	-6,409	-15,858
PBGC Premium Payment Acceleration	0	0	0	0	0	0	0	3,088	-3,088	-5,005	0	-5,005
Total	-1,196	-1,202	-1,210	-1,294	-1,507	-1,625	-1,705	1,542	-5,326	-7,340	-6,409	-20,863

Justification

PBGC provides pension insurance for private sector defined benefit retirement plans through single-employer and multiemployer programs. PBGC collects premiums that are set by the Congress separately for each of the programs. Under the multiemployer insurance program, when a plan runs out of money, PBGC provides financial assistance to the plan so that the plan can pay benefits at no more than the guarantee level.

While the single-employer program is on the path towards solvency, the multiemployer program, covering over 10 million participants, is in dire financial condition. The 2016 multiemployer program deficit was $58.8 billion, with only $2.2 billion in assets and $61 billion in liabilities. PBGC projects the multiemployer program will be insolvent by the end of 2025, at which point participants in insolvent plans would see their benefits cut by as much as 90 percent. Multiemployer premiums are very low-a flat rate of just $28 per participant in 2017. In order to better align multiemployer premiums with the risk PBGC is insuring and prevent insolvency, the Budget proposes to create a variable-rate premium (VRP)-as exists in the single-employer program-and an exit premium.

The multiemployer VRP would require plans to pay an additional premium based on their level of underfunding, up to a cap. Premiums would be indexed to inflation, with additional rate increases imposed in 2022 and 2027. PBGC would have limited authority to design waivers for terminated plans, or plans that are in critical status, if there is a substantial risk that the payment of premiums would accelerate plan insolvency and result in earlier financial assistance.

An exit premium, equal to 10 times the flat-rate premium, would be assessed on employers that withdraw from a plan to compensate the insurance program for the additional risk imposed on it when employers leave the system and cease making plan contributions. Employers who withdraw from a multiemployer plan pay a withdrawal liability to the plan, but this payment is typically insufficient to cover the employer's share of the plan's unfunded liabilities.

UNEMPLOYMENT INSURANCE SOLVENCY STANDARD
Department of Labor

Despite several years of recovery since the recession, State Unemployment Insurance (UI) programs are still not adequately financed. Fewer than half the States have sufficient reserves to weather a single year of recession, the common measure of trust fund solvency. The Budget proposes to add a minimum solvency standard to address the challenge States face in maintaining sufficient reserves in their Unemployment Trust Fund accounts to weather future recessions.

Funding Summary
(In millions of dollars)

	2018	2019	2020	2021	2022	2023	2024	2025	2026	2027	2018-22	2018-27
Proposed Change from Current Law........................	0	0	-758	-1,894	-2,568	-1,045	-1,833	-1,072	-1,488	-2,254	-5,220	-12,912

Justification

States are expected to build up sufficient reserves in their Unemployment Insurance (UI) programs during non-recessionary periods to allow them to pay for benefits during the next recession. When States fail to build up sufficient balances, they either need to increase taxes on employers in the middle of a recession or borrow from the Federal Government, which can trigger increased taxes on employers through automatic Federal Unemployment Tax Act (FUTA) "credit reductions."

Currently, fewer than half the States have sufficient reserves to cover a full year of benefits during a recession-the common measure of State solvency in the UI program. The Budget proposes to encourage States to build up reserves in their Unemployment Trust Fund accounts by implementing a minimum solvency standard, equal to the level of reserves that would be sufficient to pay six months of benefits during an average recession (half of the common solvency target). This proposal would impose credit reductions on States that fail to meet the solvency standard for two consecutive years rather than only imposing the credit reduction once States have been borrowing from the Federal Government for two consecutive years. This would strengthen States' incentive to adequately fund their UI systems, before their Trust Funds face any future recessionary demands, resulting in a decrease in the likelihood of insolvency and the need to borrow. All funds received through the credit reduction would be applied to State Unemployment Trust Fund accounts to help States rebuild balances.

AUTHORITY FOR BUREAU OF ENGRAVING AND PRINTING TO CONSTRUCT A NEW FACILITY

Department of the Treasury

The Budget proposes to provide authority to the Bureau of Engraving and Printing (BEP) to construct a more efficient production facility.

Funding Summary
(In millions of dollars)

	2018	2019	2020	2021	2022	2023	2024	2025	2026	2027	2018-22	2018-27
Proposed Change from Current Law..........................	-15	-74	-3	5	-314	5	14	3	165	-494	-401	-708

Justification

BEP's current production facility in Washington, D.C. is an aging and outdated building that cannot accommodate the basic requirements of modern currency production and requires costly renovations. Purchasing and constructing a new facility would be less expensive and would make the manufacturing process more efficient. However, under current law, BEP does not have the authority to purchase or construct a new production facility. This proposal would allow BEP to purchase and construct a new facility, resulting in savings to the Federal Government.

REQUIRE SSN FOR CHILD TAX CREDIT & EARNED INCOME TAX CREDIT
Department of the Treasury

The Budget proposes requiring a Social Security Number (SSN) that is valid for work in order to claim the Earned Income Tax Credit (EITC) or the Child Tax Credit (CTC). For both credits, this requirement would apply to taxpayers, spouses, and all qualifying children. Under current law, households who do not have SSNs that are valid for work, including illegal immigrants who use Individual Taxpayer Identification Numbers, can claim the CTC, including the refundable portion. This proposal would ensure that only individuals who are authorized to work in the United States could claim these credits.

Funding Summary
(In millions of dollars)

	2018	2019	2020	2021	2022	2023	2024	2025	2026	2027	2018-22	2018-27
Proposed Change from Current Law..........................	-449	-4,512	-4,447	-4,358	-4,309	-4,296	-4,373	-4,460	-4,555	-4,652	-18,075	-40,411

Justification

The Budget would ensure that only people who are authorized to work in the United States receive the EITC and CTC. Under current law, households who do not have SSNs that are valid for work, including illegal immigrants who use Individual Taxpayer Identification Numbers, can claim the child tax credit, including the refundable portion. This proposal would also fix gaps in the current administrative practice for EITC filers that allowed some people who have SSNs that are not valid for work to still claim the EITC. Since the EITC is a work support, only those people who are lawfully eligible to work in the United States should be able to claim it.

CAP GI BILL FLIGHT TRAINING
Department of Veterans Affairs

Under the Post-9/11 GI Bill, the Department of Veterans Affairs (VA) pays full tuition and fees for eligible veterans at public institutions of higher learning. Some flight training programs offered through these universities (often at private, contracted schools) are much more expensive than other courses of study, often surpassing the maximum private school benefit level provided by the GI Bill. This proposal would cap the maximum benefit for all VA funded flight programs at the private school benefit cap (currently about $21,000 per year).

Funding Summary
(In millions of dollars)

	2018	2019	2020	2021	2022	2023	2024	2025	2026	2027	2018-22	2018-27
Proposed Change from Current Law............	-42	-43	-46	-48	-50	-52	-54	-56	-59	-61	-229	-511

Justification

The Post-9/11 GI Bill provides eligible veterans with full tuition and fees at public universities, and tuition and fees at private universities up to a cap of about $21,000 a year. Over the past several years, certain public schools have been offering flight training, often through contracts with private institutions, at a cost significantly higher than other courses of study. Capping the benefit at the maximum benefit provided for private schools would maintain a robust benefit but would reduce the likelihood that VA would pay excessive amounts for these programs. The savings from this proposal are designated to partially offset the costs of continuing the Veterans Choice Program.

COST OF LIVING ADJUSTMENTS ROUND DOWN
Department of Veterans Affairs

For nearly 15 years, until 2013, the Department of Veterans Affairs (VA) rounded down payment rates to all disability compensation beneficiaries. This proposal would reestablish the practice of rounding down to the nearest dollar the annual Cost Of Living Adjustments (COLA) for service-connected disability compensation, dependency and indemnity compensation, and certain education programs.

Funding Summary
(In millions of dollars)

	2018	2019	2020	2021	2022	2023	2024	2025	2026	2027	2018-22	2018-27
Proposed Change from Current Law	-20	-66	-127	-182	-235	-295	-347	-403	-466	-536	-630	-2,677

Justification

Each year, veterans in receipt of certain disability benefits receive a yearly COLA increase to ensure that the purchasing power of VA benefits is not eroded by inflation. For nearly 15 years, until 2013, the VA rounded down payment rates to all disability compensation beneficiaries. This proposal would reinstate that round-down, which has only a minimal impact, estimated at no more than $12 per year on individual veterans. The savings from this proposal are designated to partially offset the costs of continuing the Veterans Choice Program.

INDIVIDUAL UNEMPLOYABILITY
Department of Veterans Affairs

Veterans receive disability compensation based on disabling conditions incurred during military service. In addition to the benefits provided for these disabling conditions, some veterans are deemed unable to engage in any substantial work as a result of their service and receive supplemental "Individual Unemployability" benefit payments, which currently continue past Social Security retirement eligibility. This proposal would immediately halt those supplemental payments, for both current and future beneficiaries, once they reach retirement age and first become eligible for Social Security benefits. These veterans would continue to receive their basic disability benefits.

Funding Summary
(In millions of dollars)

	2018	2019	2020	2021	2022	2023	2024	2025	2026	2027	2018-22	2018-27
Proposed Change from Current Law.............	-3,205	-3,394	-3,582	-3,773	-3,968	-4,166	-4,369	-4,576	-4,787	-5,002	-17,922	-40,822

Justification

The Department of Veterans Affairs (VA) currently provides additional disability compensation benefits to veterans, irrespective of age, who it deems unable to obtain or maintain gainful employment due to their service-connected disabilities through a program called Individual Unemployability (IU). The IU program is a part of VA's disability compensation program that allows VA to pay certain veterans disability compensation at the 100 percent rate, even though VA has not rated their service-connected disabilities at the total level. These veterans have typically received an original disability rating between zero and 100 percent. The number of beneficiaries in receipt of IU benefits has more than tripled since 2000, growing from 112,400 to over 338,800 at the end of 2016. Approximately two-thirds of veterans granted IU in 2016 were over the age of 60.

Under this proposal, veterans eligible for Social Security retirement benefits would have their IU terminated upon reaching the minimum retirement age for Social Security purposes, or upon enactment of the proposal if the veteran is already eligible to receive Social Security retirement benefits. These veterans would continue to receive VA disability benefits based on their original disability rating. IU benefits would not be terminated for veterans who are ineligible for Social Security retirement benefits, allowing them to continue to receive IU past minimum retirement age. This proposal would reduce the duplication of benefits resulting from veterans not participating in the labor market. The savings from this proposal would be designated to partially offset the costs of continuing the Veterans Choice Program.

REFORM INLAND WATERWAYS FINANCING
Corps of Engineers

The Administration proposes to reform the laws governing the Inland Waterways Trust Fund, including establishing an annual fee to increase the amount paid by commercial navigation users of the inland waterways. In 1986, Congress provided that commercial traffic on the inland waterways would be responsible for 50 percent of the capital costs of the locks, dams, and other features that make barge transportation possible on the inland waterways. The additional revenue would help finance future capital investments in these waterways to support economic growth, since the current excise tax on diesel fuel used in inland waterways commerce will not produce the revenue needed to cover these costs.

Funding Summary
(In millions of dollars)

	2018	2019	2020	2021	2022	2023	2024	2025	2026	2027	2018-22	2018-27
Proposed Change from Current Law..........................	-108	-107	-106	-105	-104	-103	-103	-101	-100	-100	-530	-1,037

Justification

The Army Corps of Engineers (Corps) inland waterways program constructs, operates, and maintains 229 lock chambers at 187 dam sites, and other features that make it possible to move cargo by barge on 12,000 miles of developed inland channels. Nearly all of the Federal cost to support navigation on the inland waterways involves Corps spending on the locks and dams - to construct, operate, maintain, repair, replace, and rehabilitate them; and to expand the level of service that they provide. Under current law, barge owners pay 50 percent of the cost of most inland waterways capital investments (with the exception of the Olmsted Locks and Dam Project). The General Fund pays the other 50 percent of these costs, plus all of the operation and maintenance. The central financing challenge now facing the inland waterways program is that the current diesel fuel tax (which the Congress increased from 20 cents per gallon to 29 cents per gallon in 2014) will not generate enough revenue to support the user-financed 50 percent share of the capital investments that will likely be needed over the next 10 to 15 years. The current balance of the Inland Waterways Trust Fund is less than $60 million. The Budget proposes to increase revenue to support additional work on the inland waterways through a new user fee. This proposal would raise just over $1 billion over the ten year window to finance the users' share of anticipated capital investment projects on the inland waterways.

WASHINGTON AQUEDUCT DIVESTITURE
Corps of Engineers

The Budget proposes to divest the Federal Government of the Washington Aqueduct (Aqueduct), which is the wholesale water supply system for Washington, D.C.; Arlington County, Virginia; and parts of Fairfax County, Virginia.

Funding Summary
(In millions of dollars)

	2018	2019	2020	2021	2022	2023	2024	2025	2026	2027	2018-22	2018-27
Proposed Change from Current Law	0	0	-119	0	0	0	0	0	0	0	-119	-119

Justification

The Army Corps of Engineers (Corps) owns and operates the Aqueduct, which is the only local water supply system in the Nation owned and operated by the Corps. The Aqueduct's wholesale customers pay the Corps to cover the cost of routine Aqueduct operations. The Corps borrowed $75 million from the Treasury in the mid-1990s to pay for certain capital improvements (Aqueduct customers are in the process of repaying that amount to the U.S. Treasury). Ownership of local water supply is best carried out by State or local government or the private sector where there are appropriate market and regulatory incentives. The proposal to eliminate the Corps' role in local water supply and increase the State/local/private sector's role would encourage a more efficient allocation of economic resources and mitigate risk to taxpayers.

INCREASE EMPLOYEE CONTRIBUTIONS
Office of Personnel Management

This proposal would increase Federal employee contributions to the Federal Employees Retirement System (FERS), equalizing employee and employer contribution to FERS so that half of the normal cost would be paid by each. For some specific occupations, such as law enforcement officers and firefighters, the cost of their retirement package necessitates a higher normal cost percentage. For those specific occupations this proposal would increase, but not equalize, employee contributions.

This adjustment would reduce the long-term cost to the Federal Government by reducing the Government's contribution rate. To lessen the impact on employees, this proposal would be phased in over several years.

Funding Summary
(In millions of dollars)

	2018	2019	2020	2021	2022	2023	2024	2025	2026	2027	2018-22	2018-27
Proposed Change from Current Law	-1,719	-3,227	-4,810	-6,372	-7,959	-9,537	-9,568	-9,599	-9,624	-9,640	-24,087	-72,055

Note: Savings exclude non-scoreable impacts due to the loss of intragovernmental employer share receipts. Savings also do not include the Budget proposal to reduce the discretionary spending limits to reflect the reductions in normal cost contributions paid by Federal agencies.

Justification

According to an April 25, 2017 Congressional Budget Office Report[1], Federal employees are compensated with combined pay and benefits 17 percent higher than the private sector, much of which is provided in the form of benefits costs. As the CBO study shows, in comparison to the private sector, the Federal Government continues to offer a very generous package of retirement benefits even when controlling for certain characteristics of workers. At large private sector firms, only approximately 35 percent of workers at these large firms had access to a combination of defined benefit and defined contribution programs.[2]

The Administration has lessened the impact of the proposal to increase employee contribution to FERS, by phasing in the implementation with a one-percent increase in contributions each year. Thus, for 2018, the proposed 1.9 percent pay increase would offset the increase in employee retirement contributions. In the context of the broader labor environment, the Administration believes the implementation and phasing in of retirement benefit changes will not impact the Federal Government's recruiting and retention efforts.

Citations

[1] Congressional Budget Office: *Comparing the Compensation of Federal and Private-Sector Employees, 2011 to 2015,* (April 2017).

[2] Bureau of Labor Statistics: *National Compensation Survey,* (2016).

REDUCE FEDERAL RETIREMENT BENEFITS
Office of Personnel Management

This proposal would reduce Federal employee annuities, by implementing changes to the Federal Employees Retirement System (FERS) and the Civil Service Retirement System (CSRS). The proposal would eliminate cost of living adjustments (COLAs) for FERS retirees, and would reduce CSRS retiree COLAs by 0.5 percent. The proposal would also make other changes to Federal retirement, such as eliminating the FERS Special Retirement Supplement for those employees who retire before Social Security eligibility age, and changing annuity calculations to include an employee's "High-5" salary years instead of "High-3" salary years. The employee retirement landscape continues to evolve as private companies are providing less compensation in the form of retirement benefits. The shift away from defined benefit programs and cost of living adjustments for annuitants is part of that evolution. By comparison, the Federal Government continues to offer a very generous package of retirement benefits. Consistent with the goal to bring Federal retirement benefits more in line with the private sector, adjustments to reduce the long-term costs associated with these benefits are included in this proposal.

Funding Summary
(In millions of dollars)

	2018	2019	2020	2021	2022	2023	2024	2025	2026	2027	2018-22	2018-27
Eliminate FERS COLA, Reduce CSRS COLA by 0.5%	-524	-1,187	-1,892	-2,657	-3,481	-4,369	-5,322	-6,344	-7,432	-8,591	-9,741	-41,799
Other Federal retirement changes	-1,875	-2,134	-3,055	-2,617	-3,298	-3,620	-3,943	-4,383	-4,841	-5,280	-12,979	-35,046
Total	-2,399	-3,321	-4,947	-5,274	-6,779	-7,989	-9,265	-10,727	-12,273	-13,871	-22,720	-76,845

Note: Savings exclude non-scoreable impacts due to the loss of intragovernmental employer share receipts. Savings also do not include the Budget proposal to reduce the discretionary spending limits to reflect the reductions in normal cost contributions paid by Federal agencies.

Justification

According to an April 25, 2017 Congressional Budget Office Report,[1] Federal employees are compensated with combined pay and benefits 17 percent higher than the private sector, much of which is provided in the form of benefits costs. As the CBO study shows, in comparison to the private sector, the Federal Government continues to offer a very generous package of retirement benefits even when controlling for certain characteristics of workers. At large private sector firms, only approximately 35 percent of workers at these large firms had access to a combination of defined benefit and defined contribution programs.[2]

Citations

[1] Congressional Budget Office, *Comparing the Compensation of Federal and Private-Sector Employees, 2011 to 2015*, (April 2017).

[2] Bureau of Labor Statistics: *National Compensation Survey*, (2016).

ELIMINATE THE SECURITIES AND EXCHANGE COMMISSION'S RESERVE FUND
Other Independent Agencies

The Budget proposes to restore the Securities and Exchange Commission's (SEC) accountability to the American taxpayer by eliminating its Reserve Fund, created by the Dodd-Frank Wall Street Reform and Consumer Protection Act (the Dodd-Frank Act).

Funding Summary
(In millions of dollars)

	2018	2019	2020	2021	2022	2023	2024	2025	2026	2027	2018-22	2018-27
Proposed Change from Current Law..........	0	-50	-50	-50	-50	-50	-50	-50	-50	-50	-200	-450

Justification

Created by the Dodd-Frank Act, the SEC's mandatory Reserve Fund has come to represent an extension of the Agency's regular appropriation rather than the emergency reserve it was intended to be. This proposal would restore SEC's accountability by diverting Reserve Fund resources to the General Fund for deficit reduction and requiring the SEC to request any additional appropriations from the Congress.

REFORM THE POSTAL SERVICE
Other Independent Agencies

The Budget proposes to reform the United States Postal Service (USPS) to allow the agency to meet its financial and service obligations with business revenue, as intended, rather than a taxpayer-financed bailout. The reform proposal includes changes to USPS's rate setting, delivery schedule and methods, and updated health and pension costs consistent with Government-wide reforms proposed for all Federal employees.

Funding Summary
(In millions of dollars)

	2018	2019	2020	2021	2022	2023	2024	2025	2026	2027	2018-22	2018-27
Postal Reform (Postal Service Effects, Off-Budget, No PAYGO)	-510	-3,154	-2,689	-2,286	-1,977	-2,335	-1,816	-1,586	-1,342	-1,325	-10,616	-19,020
Postal Reform (OPM Effects, On-Budget, PAYGO)	-2,297	-1,531	-2,182	-2,505	-2,946	-2,569	-3,097	-3,209	-3,334	-3,330	-11,461	-27,000
Total	-2,807	-4,685	-4,871	-4,791	-4,923	-4,904	-4,913	-4,795	-4,676	-4,655	-22,077	-46,020

Justification

The USPS has reported multi-billion dollar losses since 2007, and since 2012 has prioritized payments to employees and vendors, while defaulting on $34 billion in required payments to the Office of Personnel Management (OPM) for current and former employee benefits costs.

The Budget proposes a combination of operational reforms and retiree health and pension changes to restore solvency to the Postal Service and ensure that it funds existing commitments to current and former employees from business revenues rather than taxpayer funds. Operational reforms include changes to how rates are set, modification of USPS's delivery schedule, and use of more efficient delivery methods. In addition to Government-wide changes to Health and Pension programs (see the Office of Personnel Management section), the Budget proposes specific Postal reforms designed to better align Postal benefits with Government-wide standards and more accurately reflect the true cost of Postal pensions by using demographic factors specific to Postal Service employees.

In total, the Budget estimates that these reforms will reduce the unified budget deficit by $46 billion over 10 years and result in on-budget savings of $27 billion as the Postal Service resumes statutory payments to the Retiree Health Benefits Fund and other on-budget OPM accounts.

RESTRUCTURE THE CONSUMER FINANCIAL PROTECTION BUREAU
Other Independent Agencies

The Budget proposes to restructure the Consumer Financial Protection Bureau (CFPB), limit the Agency's mandatory funding in 2018, and provide discretionary appropriations to fund the Agency beginning in 2019.

Funding Summary
(In millions of dollars)

	2018	2019	2020	2021	2022	2023	2024	2025	2026	2027	2018-22	2018-27
Proposed Change from Current Law	-145	-650	-683	-706	-726	-745	-764	-784	-804	-826	-2,910	-6,833

Justification

Restructuring the CFPB to refocus its efforts on enforcing enacted consumer protection laws is a necessary first step to scale back harmful regulatory impositions and prevent future regulatory hurdles that stunt economic growth and ultimately hurt the consumers that CFPB was originally created to protect. Furthermore, subjecting the reformed Agency to the appropriations process would provide the oversight necessary to impose financial discipline and prevent future overreach of the Agency into consumer advocacy and activism.

SPECTRUM LICENSE FEE
Other Independent Agencies

The Budget proposes to provide the Federal Communications Commission (FCC) with new authority to use economic mechanisms, such as fees, as a spectrum management tool.

Funding Summary
(In millions of dollars)

	2018	2019	2020	2021	2022	2023	2024	2025	2026	2027	2018-22	2018-27
Proposed Change from Current Law	-50	-150	-300	-450	-500	-500	-500	-500	-500	-500	-1,450	-3,950

Justification

To promote the efficient use of the electromagnetic spectrum, the Administration proposes to provide the Federal Communications Commission (FCC) with new authority to use economic mechanisms, such as fees, as a spectrum management tool. The FCC would be authorized to set user fees on unauctioned spectrum licenses based on spectrum-management principles. Fees would be phased in over time as part of an ongoing rulemaking process to determine the appropriate application and level for fees that maximizes spectrum utilization.

U.S. GOVERNMENT PUBLISHING OFFICE
Keeping America Informed | OFFICIAL | DIGITAL | SECURE

Budget of the U.S. Government, FY 2018
Stock #: 041-001-00723-7
ISBN #: 978-0-16-093922-8
Price: $38.00

Appendix-Budget of the U.S. Government, FY 2018
Stock #: 041-001-00720-2
ISBN #: 978-0-16-093933-4
Price: $79.00

Analytical Perspectives-Budget of the U.S. Government, FY 2018
Stock #: 041-001-00721-1
ISBN #: 978-0-16-093934-1
Price: $56.00

Major Savings and Reforms, Budget of the U.S. Government Fiscal Year 2018
Stock #: 041-001-00724-5
ISBN #: 978-0-16-093945-7
Price: $35.00

CD-ROM / Budget of the U.S. Government, FY 2018
Stock #: 041-001-00722-9
ISBN #: 978-0-16-093935-8
Price: $29.00

U.S. GOVERNMENT PUBLISHING OFFICE
Keeping America Informed | OFFICIAL | DIGITAL | SECURE

Order Processing Code: 3620

Easy Secure Internet: bookstore.gpo.gov

Toll Free: 866 512–1800
DC Area: 202 512–1800
Fax: 202 512–2104

Mail: US Government Publishing Office
P.O. Box 979050
St. Louis, MO 63197–9000

Qty	Stock Number	ISBN Number	Publication Title	Unit Price	Total Price
	041-001-00723-7	978-0-16-093922-8	Budget of the U.S. Government, FY 2018	$38.00	
	041-001-00720-2	978-0-16-093933-4	Appendix-Budget of the U.S. Government, FY 2018	$79.00	
	041-001-00721-1	978-0-16-093934-1	Analytical Perspectives-Budget of the U.S. Government, FY 2018	$56.00	
	041-001-00724-5	978-0-16-093945-7	Major Savings and Reforms, Budget of the U.S. Government Fiscal Year 2018	$35.00	
	041-001-00722-9	978-0-16-093935-8	CD ROM / Budget of the U.S. Government, FY 2018	$29.00	
				Total Order	

Personal Name (Please type or Print)

Company Name

Street Address

City, State, Zip Code

Check Method of Payment

☐ Check payable to *Superintendent of Documents*
☐ SOD Deposit Account
☐ VISA ☐ MasterCard ☐ Discover/NOVUS ☐ American Express

(EXPIRATION DATE)

Thank you for your order!

Daytime Phone Including Area Code

AUTHORIZING SIGNATURE

05/17

U.S. GOVERNMENT PUBLISHING OFFICE
Keeping America Informed | OFFICIAL | DIGITAL | SECURE

Budget of the U.S. Government, FY 2018
Stock #: 041-001-00723-7
ISBN #: 978-0-16-093922-8
Price: $38.00

Appendix-Budget of the U.S. Government, FY 2018
Stock #: 041-001-00720-2
ISBN #: 978-0-16-093933-4
Price: $79.00

Analytical Perspectives-Budget of the U.S. Government, FY 2018
Stock #: 041-001-00721-1
ISBN #: 978-0-16-093934-1
Price: $56.00

Major Savings and Reforms, Budget of the U.S. Government Fiscal Year 2018
Stock #: 041-001-00724-5
ISBN #: 978-0-16-093945-7
Price: $35.00

CD-ROM / Budget of the U.S. Government, FY 2018
Stock #: 041-001-00722-9
ISBN #: 978-0-16-093935-8
Price: $29.00

U.S. GOVERNMENT PUBLISHING OFFICE
Keeping America Informed | OFFICIAL | DIGITAL | SECURE

Order Processing Code: 3620
Easy Secure Internet: bookstore.gpo.gov
Toll Free: 866 512–1800
DC Area: 202 512–1800
Fax: 202 512–2104
Mail: US Government Publishing Office
P.O. Box 979050
St. Louis, MO 63197–9000

Qty	Stock Number	ISBN Number	Publication Title	Unit Price	Total Price
	041-001-00723-7	978-0-16-093922-8	Budget of the U.S. Government, FY 2018	$38.00	
	041-001-00720-2	978-0-16-093933-4	Appendix-Budget of the U.S. Government, FY 2018	$79.00	
	041-001-00721-1	978-0-16-093934-1	Analytical Perspectives-Budget of the U.S. Government, FY 2018	$56.00	
	041-001-00724-5	978-0-16-093945-7	Major Savings and Reforms, Budget of the U.S. Government Fiscal Year 2018	$35.00	
	041-001-00722-9	978-0-16-093935-8	CD ROM / Budget of the U.S. Government, FY 2018	$29.00	
				Total Order	

Personal Name (Please type or Print)

Company Name

Street Address

City, State, Zip Code

Daytime Phone Including Area Code

Check Method of Payment
☐ Check payable to *Superintendent of Documents*
☐ SOD Deposit Account
☐ VISA ☐ MasterCard ☐ Discover/NOVUS ☐ American Express

(EXPIRATION DATE)

Thank you for your order!

AUTHORIZING SIGNATURE

05/17

U.S. GOVERNMENT PUBLISHING OFFICE
Keeping America Informed | OFFICIAL | DIGITAL | SECURE

Budget of the U.S. Government, FY 2018
Stock #: 041-001-00723-7
ISBN #: 978-0-16-093922-8
Price: $38.00

Appendix-Budget of the U.S. Government, FY 2018
Stock #: 041-001-00720-2
ISBN #: 978-0-16-093933-4
Price: $79.00

Analytical Perspectives-Budget of the U.S. Government, FY 2018
Stock #: 041-001-00721-1
ISBN #: 978-0-16-093934-1
Price: $56.00

Major Savings and Reforms, Budget of the U.S. Government Fiscal Year 2018
Stock #: 041-001-00724-5
ISBN #: 978-0-16-093945-7
Price: $35.00

CD-ROM / Budget of the U.S. Government, FY 2018
Stock #: 041-001-00722-9
ISBN #: 978-0-16-093935-8
Price: $29.00

U.S. GOVERNMENT PUBLISHING OFFICE
Keeping America Informed | OFFICIAL | DIGITAL | SECURE

Order Processing Code: 3620
Easy Secure Internet: bookstore.gpo.gov
Toll Free: 866 512–1800
DC Area: 202 512–1800
Fax: 202 512–2104
Mail: US Government Publishing Office
P.O. Box 979050
St. Louis, MO 63197–9000

Qty	Stock Number	ISBN Number	Publication Title	Unit Price	Total Price
	041-001-00723-7	978-0-16-093922-8	Budget of the U.S. Government, FY 2018	$38.00	
	041-001-00720-2	978-0-16-093933-4	Appendix-Budget of the U.S. Government, FY 2018	$79.00	
	041-001-00721-1	978-0-16-093934-1	Analytical Perspectives-Budget of the U.S. Government, FY 2018	$56.00	
	041-001-00724-5	978-0-16-093945-7	Major Savings and Reforms, Budget of the U.S. Government Fiscal Year 2018	$35.00	
	041-001-00722-9	978-0-16-093935-8	CD ROM / Budget of the U.S. Government, FY 2018	$29.00	
				Total Order	

Personal Name _____ (Please type or Print)

Company Name _____

Street Address _____

City, State, Zip Code _____

Check Method of Payment

☐ Check payable to *Superintendent of Documents*

☐ SOD Deposit Account ☐☐☐☐☐☐☐ — ☐

☐ VISA ☐ MasterCard ☐ Discover/NOVUS ☐ American Express

(EXPIRATION DATE)

Thank you for your order!

Daytime Phone Including Area Code

AUTHORIZING SIGNATURE

05/17

ISBN 978-0-16-093945-7